E-commerce Law:

National and Transnational Topics and Perspectives

E-commerce Law:

National and Transnational Topics and Perspectives

edited by

Professor H. Snijders
and
Professor S. Weatherill

KLUWER LAW INTERNATIONAL
THE HAGUE / LONDON / NEW YORK

A C.I.P. Catalogue record for this book is available from the Library of Congress.

ISBN 90 411 9917 9

Published by Kluwer Law International,
P.O. Box 85889, 2508 CN The Hague, The Netherlands.
sales@kluwerlaw.com
http://www.kluwerlaw.com

Sold and distributed in North, Central and South America
by Aspen Publishers, Inc.
7201 McKinney Circle, Frederick, MD 21704, USA

Sold and distributed in all other countries
by Turpin Distribution Services Limited,
Blackhorse Road, Letchworth, Herts,
SG6 1HN, United Kingdom

Printed on acid-free paper

Printed in the Netherlands.

Contents

Abbreviations

AC	Appeal Cases
ALL ER	All England Law Reports
AMI	Tijdschrift voor Auteurs-, Media, en Informatierecht
AOL	America Online
Bb	Bedrijfsjuridische Berichten
Buxton LJ	Buxton Law Journal
BW	Burgerlijk Wetboek
CDE	Cahiers de Droit Européen
Cir	Circuit
CMLRev	Common Market Law Review
Con LR	Construction Law Reports
CSP	Certification Service Provider
DDC	District Court for the District of Columbia
DSL	Digital Subscriber Line
EC	European Community
ECP.NL	Electronic Commerce Platform Netherlands
ECR	European Courts Review
EEC	European Economic Community
EIPR	European Intellectual Property Review
ELJ	Electronic Law Journals
ELRev	European Law Review
ETSI	Europese Telecommunicatie Standaardisatie Instituut
EU	European Union
EWCA (civ)	Court of Appeal, Civil Division (England and Wales)
HC	High Court
HR	Hoge Raad
HTML	Hyper Text Markup Language
XML	Extensible Markup Language
EDI	Electronic Data Interchange
KG	Kort Geding
ICANN	Internet Corporation for Assigned Names and Numbers
ICC	International Chamber of Commerce
IER	Intellectuele Mededingingsautoriteit
IT	Information Technology
JEPP	Journal of European Public Policy
LQR	Law Quarterly Review
Media L Rep	Media Law Reporter

MJ	Maastricht Journal of European and Comparative Law
NGO	Non Governmental Organisation
NJ	Nederlandse Jurisprudentie
NMA	Nederlandse Mededingingsautoriteit
NTBR	Nederlands Tijdschrift voor Burgerlijk Recht
NVM	Nederlandse Vereniging van Makelaars o.g. en Vastgoed-deskundigen
NY Sup ct	New York Supreme Court
OJ	Official Journal of the European Community
OPTA	Onafhankelijke Post en Telecommunicatie Autoriteit
PbEG/PB	Publicatieblad van de Europese Gemeenschappen (Dutch version of the Official Journal of the European Community, OJ)
QB	Queen's Bench Division
QBB	Queen's Bench, Divisional Court
RabelsZ	Rabels Zeitschrift
RTDE	Revue Trimestrielle de Droit Européen
SEW	Sociaal-Economische Wetgeving
SGML	Standard Generalized Markup Language
SI	Statutory Instrument
Stb	Staatsblad
TLR	Times Law Reports
TTP	Trusted Third Party
UML	Unified Modelling Language
UN/Edifact	United Nations Rules for Electronic Date Interchange for Administration, Commerce and Transport
UNCITRAL	United Nations Commission on International Trade
UNIDROIT	International Institute for the Unification of Private Law
USC	United State Code
USDC	United States District Court
WLR	Weekly Law Reports
WPNR	Weekblad voor Privaatrecht, Notariaat Registratie
WTP	World Trade Organisation
Yale LJ	Yale Law Journal

Preface

This book may be considered as a reproduction, elaboration and updating of the results of the first staff exchange between the Universities of Oxford and Leiden in the new millennium (Leiden 2001): papers on e-commerce prepared by legal experts from both sides of the North Sea have been elaborated and updated for a broader audience.

A key feature of this book is that e-commerce is not dealt with as a separate subject of law. After all, it is not a closed shop; on the contrary. That is why the authors focus on many different areas of supranational and national civil law, both on the classical ones and on relatively new fields of law such as IT law and intellectual property law. The common thread is found in the aim of the research: to analyse the meaning of the relevant field of law for e-commerce.

We are most grateful to Mirjam Sombroek-van Doorm and her management assistants, Riekje Boumlak and Karin van Heijningen (E.M. Meijers Instituut, Leiden University), for the organisation of the staff exchange and their organisational support of this publication, to Dev Saif Gangjee (Lady Margaret Hall, Oxford University) for assisting Robert Stevens with his contribution, to Joosje Brouwer and Brigitte Koet-van der Werff (Civil law division of Leiden University) for their secretarial assistance, to Elout Korevaar (former research assistant of the Civil law division of Leiden University) for his organisational support of this publication, to Dennis Horeman and Christine Vreede (research assistants of the Civil law division of Leiden University) for the editorial support and the compilation of the subject index, to Benjamin Ruijsenaars (legal translator) for the comments on the English texts of the Dutch authors and to Birgit van den Hoven and Iris Toussaint (of the Leiden company TGV teksten en presentaties) for (i.a.) lay-outing and controlling the consistency of the book. Last but not least, we are deeply indebted to the Europaeum for its generous financial support to both the staff exchange and the publication of this collection of contributions. We believe our Anglo-Dutch collaboration to be firmly in the tradition and ambition of the Euroapeum to promote and extend scholarly exchange of views in Europe.

Henk Snijders and Stephen Weatherill (editors) — Leiden/Oxford, 5 December 2002

General introduction

Henk Snijders and Stephen Weatherill

1 The importance of being e-commerce

The subject of e-commerce is undoubtedly one of the most fascinating and topical subjects of legal research in Britain, in the Netherlands, in Europe, in today's world. This sounds like a commercial. Indeed, we are quoting the advertisement text of the Leiden-Oxford staff exchange flyer, which has provided the basis for the contributions to this book, but it is not only a question of advertising. E-commerce is subject to rulings at the transnational level of the European Union, the United Nations Commission on International Trade Law and the International Chamber of Commerce, for instance. It was one of the main topics of the ICC Conference in Budapest in the year 2000 and the (main) topic of many other conferences in the recent past. It is truly a modern topic of major impact. Nonetheless its nuances are far from fully understood. Accordingly we are convinced there remain a lot of legal and policy problems connected with e-commerce that suffice to justify a staff exchange of legal experts from Leiden and Oxford devoted to research into the matter. Another good argument for the choice of e-commerce may be that, although the subject is a separate one for specialisation in law firms, for instance, it is an extremely multi-dimensional subject that requires the special attention of experts in many branches of law. In fact, almost every legal area is in some way involved. Thus, there are more than enough good reasons for legal experts from both countries involved to focus on this subject from their particular expert viewpoint and to try and thrash out the tangled ball of e-commerce.

2 What holds off line, holds on line, but ...

For all authors the starting point can be that what holds off line, holds on line, because we cannot conceivably afford or accept completely different laws for e-commerce on the one hand and other forms of commerce on the other hand. Most considerations in this collection of contributions can, indeed, be seen to be built around this core assumption. However, there are a lot of exceptions to the rule of thumb just mentioned and the considerations in this collection are equally illustrative of this point. This already provides an enticing glimpse of the intellectual excitement of examining the regulation of e-commerce.

First of all, we can observe that the law governing e-commerce and other on-line communications develop more or less independently of other law through suprana-

H. Snijders, S. Weatherill (eds.), *E-commerce Law*, 1-8

tional and international incentives. These incentives do not come only from the public organisations authorised to make law, such as UNCITRAL and the European Union, but also from organisations in private practice such as the International Chamber of Commerce. For example, we mention the UNCITRAL Model Law on Electronic Signatures, the European Directive on the protection of Consumers in respect of Distance Contracts (Directive 97/7) and the European Directive on E-commerce (Directive 2000/31) respectively the ICC Draft Uniform Rules for Electronic Trade and Settlement. These supranational and international developments are not so astonishing or even surprising, for the making of uniform (model) law seems simpler when domestic law is lacking or at least inadequately developed or incomplete and there is accordingly a need for legislation anyway. The intellectual interest, of course, lies not simply in the fact that legislation is proliferating, nor that there are multiple sources of lawmaking. E-commerce, as an economic activity capable of being pursued in a technologically border-free environment, has prompted the growth of a web of multi-level, national and transnational rule-making in response. This is a classic case of economic and technological change which forces lawyers – be they lawmakers, practitioners or academic lawyers – to ponder how overlapping sources of national and transnational law can be shaped to cope with the challenge of rapid and unpredictable market developments. E-commerce, then, is fascinating in its own right from the legal perspective but, on a broader scale, it offers an intriguing case study of the limitations and possibilities for moulding an effective governance regime involving many different lawmakers, national and transnational, public and private, designed to regulate but not to damage the growth of an emerging sector of the economy.

Another observation may be that off-line law often entails difficulties when we try to apply it to on-line situations. Section 6.5.3 of the Netherlands Civil Code [Burgerlijk Wetboek (BW)], for instance, provides for use of and protection against general contract conditions that are unreasonably onerous, but how does our legislator define general conditions? Up until now, article 6:231 sub a BW defines them as 'written stipulations which have been drafted to be included into a number of contracts', so what about the use of and the protection against electronic general conditions? It is true that there is a bill pending in parliament serving to implement the European Directive on E-commerce, which therefore (in the light of article 9 of this Directive) provides for removal of the word 'written' in article 6:231 sub a BW. Removal of this word will not solve all problems, though. How, for instance, should we deal with article 6:233 sub b BW (in connection with article 6:234 BW) stating (respectively elaborating) that the user has to afford the other party a reasonable opportunity to take cognisance of the general conditions in an e-commerce context? Thus, is it sufficient if the consumer, before contracting, can find the general conditions to be applied by using a hyperlink, supposing that these general conditions can be downloaded and remain accessible for reading later on, as article 6:227 para. 4 of the bill in connection with article 10 para. 3 of the Directive requires? Some Dutch authors think that such a hyperlink would possibly not be sufficient, in particular because of the downloadability requirement of the intended new provision of article 6:234 para.1 sub c. At least one other Dutch expert is of the opinion that such a hyperlink perfectly adequately meets the requirements of the bill in connection with the Directive. We are of the same opinion, albeit that the hyperlink must clearly take part in the normal process that the consumer has to pass through before being able to give his or her permission for the e-commerce contract. If that is the case, the hyperlink can be considered as a reasonable possibility to permit the reading of the general conditions by the consumer, still supposing the electronic context of intended e-commerce transactions, of course.

Furthermore, we can observe that there are a lot of questions that arise only in the on-line area. Let us refer to the moment of effectiveness of an e-mail notice, for instance an offer to contract or its acceptance. The majority of European legal systems – this does not apply to England and Wales – generally use the receipt rule. This rule holds that a notice becomes effective as from the moment of receipt by the addressee. The same applies to article 24 of the United Nations Convention on Contracts for the International Sale of Goods, article 1.9 of the UNIDROIT Principles for International Commercial Contracts and article 2:205 of the Lando Principles of Contract Law by the Lando Commission, and – at least in this context – article 11 of the European Directive on e-commerce. But how is one to use and interpret that receipt rule in the on-line area? Supposing that the addressee uses an external e-mailbox, at what moment will the notice be effective then: the moment of receipt in the e-mailbox or the moment of receipt in the addressee's computer? This question is a typically thorny on-line question, which is under discussion in one of the contributions to this book. An example like this one clearly shows that the off-line-is-on-line doctrine may be useful, but that we cannot confine ourselves to this.

Thus, there is not just one thread in this book, but there are two: allegiance to the criterion of 'what holds off line, holds on line' on the one hand, and recognition of typical and perhaps peculiar (legal or empirical) characteristics of questions of e-commerce law and other IT law requiring special provisions and exceptions on the other hand. The predominant principle here is the methodological rule that differentiation of law always demands justification.

Actually, this conclusion is far-reaching for the organisation of legal research and education on IT law in general and e-commerce law in particular: we can no longer leave these subjects to specialists only. Generalists in branches of law such as contract law and tort law have to cooperate with experts on IT law including e-commerce law in order to achieve the most satisfying and rational legal results. Moreover, our approach also insists on the necessary collaboration of national and transnational lawyers, in order to ensure a full and adequately rich understanding of the required legal solutions. National private lawyers cannot work in a vacuum. They must engage seriously with the transnational context of economic activity and, increasingly, of law-making. Solutions that may seem appropriate according to national tradition may need to bargained for more actively, even aggressively, in the transnational domain as the rules of the EU, and other relevant actors, are agreed and then subjected to judicial interpretation. Equally, it is not open to transnational lawyers such as EC trade lawyers to apply their rules without a sympathetic and informed attitude to national rules that are subjected to the influence of European trade integration. To 'harmonise' national laws is also to (re-)create rules at European level, and it is incumbent on European lawyers to understand the full legal and cultural context of the national private law systems that are being opened up to adaptation and evolution under the influence of the growth of transnational legal rules for a transnational economy. E-commerce, then, is a subject which offers vivid opportunities for drawing together scholars from different, but converging, intellectual domains. This book is designed to reflect but also to encourage those trends.

3 OVERVIEW OF THE CONTRIBUTIONS TO THIS BOOK

A first impression of the contributions to this book, their results in themselves and in their reciprocal connection may be useful for the readers.

The book starts, more or less evidently, with an EU law approach by Stephen Weatherill.

According to the country-of-origin principle, the home State (the State where the trader is located) is predominant vis-à-vis the host State (the State of the market to which the trader wants to get access). This means that primary EC law contains a preference for home State control in the sense that a host State is entitled to apply its local rules in a manner that obstructs trade originating in other Member States only provided it is able to demonstrate a sufficiently strong justification for those rules – a 'mandatory requirement' or, more generally, a reason of sufficient weight serving the public interest. This pattern of 'home State control' is taken over into secondary legislation including the European Directive on e-commerce. This requires the e-trader's home State to enforce defined standards of good conduct relating to, for example, the provision of information to consumers, and, in return, the host State is required to allow e-traders to operate in its market without subjection to further requirements imposed within the field coordinated by the Directive. The distribution of competence between home and host States is central to understanding the techniques used both under the Treaty and under secondary legislation to pursue the quest for minimising inefficient dual regulation in the European market. For e-commerce, more than for most sectors, it will be intriguing to observe whether the law is able to meet the expectations of technological change.

One of the central items of the topic of e-commerce is the electronic signature. Rob van Esch gives a survey of rulings on electronic signature. He discusses both the European Directive on electronic signatures (1999/93) and domestic legislation in the United Kingdom and the Netherlands.

First of all Van Esch gives some examples of electronic signatures and descriptions of their underlying technologies. Then he presents an outline of the most relevant provisions of the European Directive on electronic signatures followed by a comparative analysis of the implementation of these provisions into the domestic legislation of the United Kingdom and the Netherlands. Although the harmonisation of the laws of the Member States is one of the important objectives of European Directives, Van Esch must conclude that the United Kingdom and the Netherlands have each taken a different approach to implementing the European Directive on electronic signatures. However, this does not necessarily mean that the laws of both countries deviate sharply from each other, because of the aim of interpretation of domestic laws in conformity with European Directives.

Cyril van der Net deals with civil liability of Internet providers following the European Directive on electronic commerce. Exceptions to liability such as mere conduit, caching and hosting, the absence of a general monitoring obligation and the possibility of a prohibitory injunction in these cases are at stake as well. Furthermore, this author discusses the almost complete exclusion of liability of an Internet provider who merely serves as a serving hatch, and this very critically. Some other items under review are: compensations claims, declarative judgements and the country-of-origin principle (dealt with in detail by Stephen Weatherill).

Roderick Bagshaw concentrates on four issues of tort in an on-line context, that is to say three issues of on-line tort in general and one issue of tort in the context of e-commerce in particular: the question how far those offering advice or professional services electronically will be subject to tort liability for negligence; the question how the English law of tort will deal with defective electronic products; the liability for culpable encouragement of wrongdoing by others and culpable failure to control others; and torts involving damage to e-businesses.

Bagshaw concludes inter alia that the balance between the benefits of easy access to information and the need to protect vulnerable consumers will be difficult for courts to perfect. He also observes that there is currently uncertainty as to the legal regime applicable to the producers and distributors of defective software, at least in so far as that software causes damage to persons other than those in contractual privity with their preferred defendant, and makes a contribution to the solution of this problem. Like other businesses, e-businesses will be vulnerable to damage by defamation, malicious falsehood, deceit, passing off, and a host of specialised torts. In the author's opinion the torts that may raise the most interesting questions, however, are likely to be the general torts – negligence, dealing with careless damage, and interference with trade by unlawful means, dealing with deliberate harm – and that is why he focusses mainly on these torts. One general conclusion is quite obvious: the adaptation of traditional tort doctrine to cyberworld will not be as straightforward as 'downloading' doctrine from off-line contexts.

The moment of effectiveness of e-mail notices is under discussion in the contribution by Henk Snijders.

When does the e-mail notice reach the adressee and, in particular, is receipt of the notice decisive? And if so, which corrections of and exceptions to the receipt rule have to be made? And do we choose the mailbox receipt rule or the computer receipt rule?

After some general considerations on these questions in an off-line situation respectively an on-line situation, the author analyses four specific problems of the (moment of) effectiveness of e-mail notices.

Hans Nieuwenhuis' 'Caveat emptor in digital times' deals with e-commerce and contract law. Nieuwenhuis discusses the significance of more or less classical principles and rules for contractual relations in the context of e-commerce.

What about the principle of good faith and fair dealing in this context? And can we really qualify an e-commerce transaction with a consumer as a contract, knowing that the consumer has the right to withdraw from it by his own authority? And if so, and if the delivery on the basis of such a contract implies transfer of ownership, then what are we to think of the consumer who withdraws the contract, refuses to transfer back to the trader and goes bankrupt? Must the trustee in bankruptcy still transfer back?

Josh Holmes and Bronwen Morgan use quite another approach. They emphasise the Internet's potential to operate as a self-constituting or spontaneous order in which individual human endeavours combine, without the agency of any central system of coordination, to produce a workable and mutually advantageous network of interactions.

These authors suggest that e-commerce provides a qualitatively novel context for thinking through long-familiar tensions between the promise and peril of spontaneous interaction. The novelty of this context provides grounds for qualified optimism over new ways of combining different modes of governance in the pursuit of socially optimal outcomes. What is new about the Internet as an essential service is that it is not so much a precondition for effective participation in social settings (including markets), but it is itself a zone of participation, a social setting where agency and autonomy can flourish. For this reason, policies that promote access to the Internet have more promise of establishing linkages with spontaneous modes of social interaction, and are perhaps less subject to the concerns about paternalism that state-imposed regulatory intervention so often brings in its train. In tandem with the qualified optimism about the substantive aspects of the Internet as a novel zone of commerce come provisional views that traditional top-down modes of governance are neither necessary nor appropriate in such a setting, while at the same time, 'pure spontaneity' is equally undesirable. Any approach to establishing a regulatory framework for e-commerce should build initially upon broad principles. Such principles could be binding in the context of access but non-binding in case of providing a supportive infrastructure for socially responsible consumption frameworks. The use of broad principles would also provide the limited constraints on spontaneity, while still leaving space for institutional experimentation with different mixes of horizontal and vertical governance strategies. In this way, problems may be defused that could otherwise imperil the promise of spontaneity proffered by e-commerce.

Dirk Visser in this book sails between Scylla and Charybdis. For the time being, information is the only commodity that can be transferred electronically. Therefore, information, especially large quantities of valuable information contained in databases, is the (only) ideal object for electronic commerce. At the same time, valuable information contained in databases can also be copied and transferred over the Internet without any permission or control of the person or persons who have invested substantially in this information. Therefore, a certain degree of protection of databases forms the very core of the success of trading information over the Internet. The overprotection of databases could, on the other hand, be a serious impediment to the development of electronic commerce.

Robert Stevens discusses the specific problems which e-commerce gives rise to in the context of private international law.

Stevens observes that difficulties arise both in relation to deciding whether a court has jurisdiction and, if it has, as to which law it will apply. As far as the Council Regulation on jurisdiction and enforcement of judgments in civil and commercial matters is applicable, Business-to-Business dealings do not seem to give rise to problems specific to e-commerce, Business-to-Consumer dealings may, and these problems are dealt with by Stevens. Again, it is in relation to Business-to-Consumer dealings where problems in relation to the applicable law on e-commerce may arise, and Stevens deals with these problems as well. The Directive on Electronic Commerce makes no provision in relation to jurisdiction or applicable law.

Are specific private international law rules required for electronic commerce? The author concludes that in most cases the internet does not raise issues which require different treatment from other contexts; in some cases the law obviously needs to be clarified but litigation may provide satisfactory answers without further reform.

Aernout Schmidt and Hans Franken make an analysis of e-commerce in this age but also for the future.

The authors distinguish three problem fields of IT law in general and e-commerce in particular: open texture (i.e. judge-made law by interpretation), legal engineering (the adaptation of IT practices in the law office, for instance) and inherent ambiguity (issued by the difference between the physical world and cyberspace). The three perspectives represent different positions in the legal system, relevant to electronic commerce. The open-texture perspective often coincides with post hoc legal assessment, as professed by courts, magistrates, solicitors and barristers in litigation. The engineering perspective is appropriate in commerce itself, notably when an e-commerce service is being designed and deployed. The relevant legal research in e-commerce is business-oriented and ex ante concerned with modelling the service into an architecture that supports legitimate use. The responsibility risks rest prima facie on the (legal) persons designing and deploying the service, often relying upon legal advice. The latent-ambiguity perspective links tradition with times to come and belongs to litigation in some individual cases but mainly to the legislator – providing enacted rules, addressing areas that may be considered legally void.

Summarising, the authors analyse different perspectives for legal reasoning by legal professionals: the open-texture perspective for litigation, the legal engineering perspective for legal advisors and the inherent-ambiguity perspective for rule making. The authors give a unified framework of themes and chapters, providing the contextual model of an IT service and describing the basic architecture of good IT development practice. They sketch the structure of e-commerce in cyberspace, using four service levels and three business types. They also analyse the knowledge required by the legal professionals involved. For litigation professionals, they find it necessary to be knowledgeable about the legal meaning of existing IT functions. For the advising professional, they find it necessary to be knowledgeable about the legal risks that will be relevant to future IT functions. For the legislator, they find it necessary to be knowledgeable about the ethos of and principles for cyberspace. The authors expect that, ten years from now, commerce will have mainly become e-commerce and government will have mainly become e-government and that academic legal education should accommodate these needs. Even if the last of these prophecies is not fulfilled, e-commerce will remain an important and fascinating subject of supranational, international and domestic law agendas for many years, all over the world. Only a selection of today's problems to be solved could be taken under the microscope in this book, while new problems will reveal themselves in time.

The regulation of e-commerce under EC law: the distribution of competence between home States and host States as a basis for managing the internal market*

Stephen Weatherill

1 INTRODUCTION

The purpose of this contribution is to examine the framework of EC law which dictates the extent to which local rules may impede the construction of an integrated, competitive market in e-commerce for Europe (and beyond). This involves an exploration of the structure of general EC trade law, with application to the technologically intriguing and fast-moving sector of e-commerce. This contribution covers both primary law (the EC Treaty) and secondary legislation (most prominently, Directive 2000/31 on e-commerce). It does not seek to examine in any depth the intricacies of e-commerce as such; rather, it seeks to set out the applicable rules of EC law in their broader context in the belief that this provides a foundation for discussion of the extent to which e-commerce presents special problems for the EC law-maker and law-enforcer. This contribution is especially directed at exploration of the extent to which a satisfying balance may be struck between the demands of market integration in Europe and the demands of regulatory protection, which may exercise both national and Community authorities.

Accordingly, the focus of the inquiry is: What impact does European Community law exert on the competence of public authorities in the Member States to regulate commercial activity which is (in some way) carried out on 'their' territory? The field of electronic commerce provides an interesting case study of the choices made under the Community system. E-commerce is extremely well suited to the construction of marketing strategies which involve a trader located in one Member State (the 'home State') being able to access markets in other Member States (the 'host' States) without being obliged to incur costs in maintaining a physical presence in those target States. But what is the scope for 'host States' to apply their rules of market intervention, even where they may impede cross-border trade? Should compliance by an e-trader with 'home State' rules be treated as a sufficient basis for claiming an entitlement to operate in all territories in the Union? And has EC Directive 2000/31 on e-commerce resolved these tricky questions of regulatory competence? Finding satisfactory answers to these questions of law and policy is vital to the successful realisation of the ambition expressed at the Lisbon European Council of March 2001 to convert Europe into the world's most competitive and dynamic knowledge-based economy within the next ten years.

* Paper prepared in the light of discussion at the Leiden/Oxford Europaeum seminar, Leiden, May 15 – 17 2001.

H. Snijders, S. Weatherill (eds.), *E-commerce Law*, 9-26

2 PRIMARY EC LAW

Were one to permit both the trader's home State and the States in which that trader wishes to operate (the host States) to impose their regulatory rules in full on that trader, market integration in Europe would be stunted. Such a model would respect the competence of public authorities in the Member States to select their own preferred level of intervention in the market, but the weight and diversity of such burdens would impose costs on business, and would negate the whole economically efficient process of integration. Such an approach would, by requiring traders always to conform to local market conditions, hinder efficient cross-border competition; economies of scale would not be released. But the opposite extreme, whereby host State rules would be completely set aside in so far as they interfered with the opportunities of out-of-State traders wishing to exploit host State markets, would concede too much to private market power at the expense of legitimate concerns of (national) public authorities in the host State. Indeed, the Court insists that home State supervision 'is not a principle laid down by the Treaty'.[1] Accordingly, a more sophisticated model has been devised. This allows a balance to be struck between, on the one hand, the claims of public authorities in the (host) Member States to assert regulatory preferences even where they may damage the interests of traders from other (home) Member States seeking to penetrate their markets, and, on the other, the general interest in restructuring markets along transnational lines in order to make the most of scarce European economic resources.

This is *Cassis de Dijon*.[2] The core of the judgment represents the Court's choice of balance between these competing interests. It serves as a statement of host State control, which is then heavily qualified by a demand that host State control be justified according to standards recognised by Community law:

> In the absence of common rules relating to the production and marketing of alcohol... it is for the [host] Member States to regulate all matters relating to the production and marketing of alcohol and alcoholic beverages on their own territory ... Obstacles to movement in the Community resulting from disparities between the national laws in question must be accepted in so far as those provisions may be recognised as being necessary in order to satisfy mandatory requirements relating in particular to the effectiveness of fiscal supervision, the protection of public health, the fairness of commercial transactions and the defence of the consumer....

In other words, the rules of the home State prevail, *unless* the host State is able to demonstrate a sufficiently compelling reason, a 'mandatory requirement',[3] for applying its rules to the imported product. Cross-border trade prevails, albeit that space is left for the possibility that the public authorities in the host State may be able to justify their regulatory choices. This approach to the distribution of competences between home and host States in the quest to construct an integrated market covering the territory of all the Member States of the Union does not go so far as to dictate that *either* one State *or* the other but never both shall be permitted to regulate a particular product or service sector, for space is allowed to a host State to justify its trade-restrictive rules

---

1 Case C-233/94 *Germany* v. *Parliament and Council* [1997] ECR I-2405, paragraph 64.

2 Case 120/78 *Rewe Zentrale* v. *Bundesmonopolverwaltung für Branntwein* [1979] ECR 649.

with the consequence that it is at least possible that dual regulation will occur. But there was no such justification in the case. Germany had no good reason to exclude French blackcurrant liqueur from its market, even though German traditions were different from those that governed the product in France. And so, under this interpretation of EC trade law, consumer choice and commercial freedom was enhanced at the expense of intervention in the market by public authorities in the host State.

The case law has subsequently taken some intriguing twists, but the Court has not deviated from its fundamental insistence that the regulatory competence of host Member States must be subjected to control under primary EC law in so far as an adequate threat to market integration is demonstrated as flowing from the application of those rules.[4] The expectation that restrictive rules must be justified has been extended beyond product markets, which were at stake in *Cassis de Dijon*, to embrace also service markets,[5] as the Court has steadily moved towards the construction of a general law governing free movement in the internal market.[6]

In some circumstances the Court has been prepared to accept that a sufficient justification exists for national rules that impede cross-border trade. Trade-restrictive regulatory diversity is not excluded; equally, depression to the lowest common denominator of regulatory protection among the Member States is not inevitable. The Court asserts that 'the fact that one Member State imposes less strict rules than another Member State does not mean that the latter's rules are disproportionate and hence incompatible with Community law'.[7] A regulating State may set tougher standards than its competitors provided they are underpinned by a justification recognised by Community law. In *Alpine Investments*,[8] a relatively unusual case because the challenged rules were those of a home State accused of restricting export trade, the Court agreed that a desire to maintain the high reputation of the quality of the financial services in the Netherlands was a sufficient reason for the imposition of stricter stan-

---

3 In fact this is a regrettably enduring poor translation of the original 'Zwingenden Erfordnisse'; better would be 'compelling interests'. The phrase 'the public interest' has been more common lately. On the question of mis-translation, S. Weatherill and P. Beaumont, *EU Law* (Penguin Books, 3rd. ed, 1999) p. 575 note 35 and on the more general phenomenon, J. Scott, 'Mandatory or Imperative Requirements in the EU and the WTO', Ch. 10 in: C. Barnard and J. Scott (eds.), *The Law of the Single European Market: Unpacking the Premises* (2002).

4 One of the most striking twists may be observed in Cases C-267 and C-268/91 *Keck and Mithouard* [1993] ECR I-6097 where the Court reconsidered what effect has to be shown on cross-border trade before a State falls under an obligation to justify its rules. Cf. N. Bernard, 'La libre circulation des marchandises, des personnes et des services dans le Traité CE sous l'angle de la compétence', 34 *CDE* 11 (1998).

5 A particularly good example is supplied by Case C-76/90 *Sager* v. *Dennemeyer* [1991] ECR I-4221.

6 See in particular the formula set out in paragraph 37 of Case C-55/94 *Gebhard* [1995] ECR I-4165 describing the limits of host State control and by implication an assumption of home State control as the norm. On patterns of convergence in the law of free movement see C. Barnard, 'Fitting the remaining pieces into the goods and persons jigsaw', 26 ELRev. 35 (2001); and for recent exploration including a comprehensive collection of the cascade of comment, see J. Snell, *Goods and Services in EC Law: a Study of the Relationship between the Freedoms* (2002).

7 E.g. Case C-3/95 *Reisebüro Broede* [1996] ECR I-6511; Case C-294/00 *Deutsche Paracelsus Schulen* judgment of 11 July 2002.

8 Case C-384/93 [1995] ECR I-1141.

dards than those applied to similar traders in other States such as the United Kingdom. In the field of goods a similar acknowledgement that States may legitimately differ in their assessment of risk may be identified in *Eyssen*.[9] The Dutch authorities were sufficiently anxious about the danger to human health presented by the use of a particular type of preservative in cheese that they introduced a ban. Other less cautious Member States were prepared to allow such additives. The Dutch ban impeded trade in cheeses manufactured in more permissive States, but the Court accepted that regulatory attitudes could legitimately vary in such circumstances and did not find the Netherlands to have acted unlawfully even though they had intervened in the market more vigorously than the norm elsewhere. So the case law reveals that national rules that restrict trade may be accepted as justified.[10]

But this is not normal. The case law displays a heavy bias in favour of deregulation, in the sense that most restrictive national rules have typically not been treated as justified. Most cases before the European Court are decided in a manner unfavourable to host State regulators with the result that trade integration is advanced and local regulatory preferences are suppressed. *Cassis* itself is such a decision. So too is the famous *Beer Purity* case,[11] in which it was ruled that strict German rules governing the permissible ingredients of *Bier* unlawfully restricted the commercial opportunities in Germany of producers brewing elsewhere according to different recipes and traditions. The result was *not* that production according to traditional German methods was no longer viable, but rather that such production would be – at long last – vulnerable to out-of-State competition. Consumer choice would expand. There is a strong deregulatory impetus in this case law, infused by a preference for the private autonomy of traders and consumers in the market over public regulation.[12] In the services sector, the *Tourist Guide* cases provide an equally powerful glimpse of the assumption that consumers are in general better served by deregulation and cross-border competition than by exclusionary local regulatory practices. The Court observed that competition between tour operators would ensure the hiring of competent guides and that accordingly a State licensing regime governing access to the profession could not be justified.[13] Consumers could take care of themselves adequately without the need for such public intervention.

The observation that most of these cases tend to be decided in a manner that favours the party challenging the national measure is probably best accompanied by the additional remark that one would hardly expect any different outcome. These decisions reflect the development of European market integration, driven by private litigants, which confronts the deadwood of centuries of regulatory tradition in all the Member States. The whole point of the exercise is regulatory renovation. From this perspective, the European Court is frequently asked to deal with the collision between, on the one hand, the making of a market for Europe and, on the other, na-

---

9 Case 53/80 [1981] ECR 409. Similarly, Case C-473/98 *Kemikalieinspektionen* v. *Toolex Alpha AB* [2000] ECR I-5681.

10 See further S. Weatherill, 'Recent case law concerning the free movement of goods: mapping the frontiers of market deregulation', 36 CMLRev. 51 (1999).

11 Case 178/84 [1987] ECR 1227.

12 Cf E.-J. Mestmaecker, 'On the Legitimacy of European Law', 58 RabelsZ 615 (1994).

13 Case C-154/89 *Commission* v. *France* [1991] ECR I-659.

tional rules introduced for once sound reasons that have generations ago lost their purpose mixed together with other national rules cherished by national producers as convenient means for insulating themselves from the threat of out-of-State competition. So the Court is in fact engaged in weeding out unrepresentative and outdated manifestations of national-level decision-making that are hostile to and inappropriate in an integrating European market of the type to which the Member States have committed themselves under the EC Treaty.[14] The setting aside of obstructive national rules serves the interests of consumers in the host State, who enjoy a wider choice in a more competitive market, and traders throughout the Community, who are able to construct an integrated marketing strategy. Under this model, one would fully expect an assertion of host State regulatory competence to be rigorously scrutinised in so far as it amounts to a plea to subordinate the interest in economic integration to the protection and preservation of local concerns. And the Court's formula, which places the burden on the regulating State to show a sufficient justification for such rules, reflects this anxiety.

In its application to the e-commerce sector, this formula dictates that rules of the host State that impede trade pursued by commercial operators based in other Member States are lawful – provided that a sufficiently strong justification is shown to exist. This requirement of justification is the limit placed by EC law on host State autonomy in an integrating market. One may readily question the technological feasibility of the effective application of host State rules in this sector, but, as matter of legal principle, it is the Court's *Cassis* formula that governs the assessment of the compatibility of host State regulation of the e-commerce sector with EC trade law. So, in principle, genuinely valuable national measures of consumer protection may be lawful even where they obstruct the creation of an integrated e-commerce market for Europe.

The implication here is that in principle the Treaty provisions on free movement can be worked hard in pursuit of a model of home State control but that host State control is acknowledged as permissible despite its trade-restrictive effect provided there is a sufficiently powerful justification. There is, then, a bargain of sorts struck between respect for the regulatory autonomy of the host State and desire to achieve the economic advantages of a restructured European market which is most easily built on a foundational principle of home State control. But these judicially-applied Treaty provisions, which control the exercise of State regulatory competence independently of any legislative intervention to establish common *Community* rules of market regulation, leave open the possibility of persisting market-fragmentation in so far as national rules are found to be justified, and, more generally, they do not offer a reliable, predictable framework of rules for an integrated European market in so far as they expect commercial operators to invest time and money in deploying EC law, if necessary by lengthy litigation with uncertain outcome, to suppress obstructive national rules. So, in building and maintaining a viable integrated market, something extra is needed to supplement the law of free movement contained in the Treaty. That extra element is the harmonisation of laws, achieved by Community legislative intervention.

---

14 See in particular the ground-breaking work of M. Poiares Maduro, *We, the Court* (Hart, 1998) which places the law of free movement in an imaginative constitutional context.

3 Patterns of harmonisation

On the simplest model of legislative harmonisation, diverse national rules are eliminated in favour of a single Community rule. The harmonised rule promotes trade integration by virtue of its uniform EC-wide application while also transplanting to European level the imperative of respect for the variety of interests that have stimulated (different forms of) regulatory intervention over time in the Member States. Here, then, there is a vertical redistribution of competence, from State-level to the Community as rule-maker. In the context of the legislative harmonisation programme, that core bargain struck between the long-standing culture of local regulatory competence and the broader quest for cross-border integration can be reshaped, within the political process where the necessary weighing of competing values may be thought to belong more comfortably than in the judicial setting discussed above.

In the field of e-commerce the most important measure of harmonisation of this type that has thus far been adopted is Directive 2000/31 on e-commerce. This is, more fully, Directive 2000/31 of the European Parliament and of the Council of 8 June 2000 on certain legal aspects of information society services, in particular electronic commerce, in the Internal Market.[15] Given background regulatory diversity among the Member States which is perceived to hinder the development of desirable patterns of cross-border e-trade, the Directive seeks to introduce common rules in the fields in which it applies. According to recital 5 of the Directive's Preamble, harmonisation eliminates the divergence between national laws that hinders the achievement of integration. It therefore seeks to provide a more reliable basis for trade in a single market than ever could be achieved by the application of the Treaty rules on free movement alone. The characteristic though awkward function of a measure of harmonisation of laws in reconciling the different approaches to regulation previously taken in the Member States within a single *communautaire* framework that is apt to lay the foundation of an integrated market is also openly reflected in the Directive's Preamble. In this vein recital 41 of Directive 2000/31 asserts that 'this Directive strikes a balance between the different interests at stake ....'.

Harmonisation is a process of integration and deregulation, in so far as (on the simplest model) fifteen diverse national regimes are reduced to one Community regime. But it is equally a process of 're-regulation' by the EC, in the sense the EC must make a choice about the *content* of the regime that it will introduce as the platform for an integrated market. Harmonisation, then, possesses a characteristic dual function. It establishes the ground rules for integration, but it also demands that attention be paid at Community level to choices between competing philosophies, styles and techniques of regulatory intervention in the market. So the harmonisation of national consumer law and national environmental law, for example, generates a need to understand such legislative action in the context of its contribution to European market-building but also as an exercise which has the effect of shaping a species of regulato-

15 OJ 2000 L178/1. For an overview see G. Pearce and N. Platten, 'Promoting the Information Society: the EU Directive on Electronic Commerce', 6 ELJ 363 (2000); A. Lopez-Tarruella, 'A European Community regulatory framework for electronic commerce' 38 CMLRev. 1337 (2001).

ry sub-discipline that may be labelled 'European consumer law'[16] or 'European environmental law'.[17] The functional breadth of the harmonisation programme 'spills over' to infuse with a European element a number of areas of regulatory activity that the Treaty seems to leave predominantly in the hands of the Member States. This is recognised by the Treaty. Article 95(3) EC, in its form effective since the Amsterdam Treaty entered into force on 1 May 1999, provides that 'The Commission, in its proposals envisaged in paragraph 1 concerning health, safety, environmental protection and consumer protection, will take as a base a high level of protection, taking account in particular of any new development based on scientific facts. Within their respective powers, the European Parliament and the Council will also seek to achieve this objective'. Moreover the 'horizontal' provisions found in Articles 6, 152 and 153(2) EC since the entry into force of the Amsterdam Treaty dictate that environmental protection, public health and consumer protection requirements shall be taken into account in defining and implementing other Community policies and activities, including, no doubt, market-building listed in Article 3 EC and elaborated in, inter alia, Article 14. In this way an association is conceded between the task of market-making and the quality of the accompanying regulatory environment.

This 're-regulatory bargain' involves the setting of common Community standards which are designed to take care of the interests of both the 'home State' and the interests of the 'host State' within the process of market integration. The choice of regulatory technique and of the appropriate level of intervention must also be blended with a distribution of competence between home and host States with regard to the application of the agreed rules. There are, in fact, two distinct issues at stake in the process of competence distribution under the programme of harmonisation. The first involves the fixing of common Community ('re-regulatory') standards that operate in the field occupied by the Directive, and which – in whole or in part – displace the competence of the States to apply different rules. This, then, is the setting of common rules for a common market, and sensitive questions of interpretation arise as to the extent to which State action is 'pre-empted'. This may be governed by the Treaty basis for the adopted legislation,[18] by the terms of the legislation itself[19] or it may fall to the Court to interpret legislation that is ambiguous or silent on the point.[20] But even when those common rules are agreed and when in principle the regulatory regime does not vary across the territory of the Union, the question also arises as to

---

16 See e.g. S. Weatherill, *EC Consumer Law and Policy* (Longman Publishing, 1997); G. Howells and T. Wilhelmsson, *EC Consumer Law* (Dartmouth Publishing, 1997).

17 See e.g. J. Scott, *EC Environmental Law* (Longman Publishing, 1998); J. Jans, *European Environmental Law* (Europa Law Publishing, 2000).

18 E.g. Art. 176 EC provides that Member States may apply stricter rules of environmental protection than are established by Community legislation. See Jans 2000, ch.III (see note 17).

19 Measures harmonising national rules governing protection of the economic interests of consumers, though made under Arts. 100 or 100a EC, now 94 or 95 EC, typically include a 'minimum' clause permitting stricter local rules; see S. Weatherill and P. Beaumont, *EU Law* (Penguin Books, 3rd ed., 1999), p.1053. On the constitutional limits of minimum harmonisation under these market-building Treaty provisions, see Case C-376/98 *Germany* v. *Parliament and Council* [2000] ECR I-8419, paras. 101-104.

20 E.g. Case 148/78 *Ratti* [1979] ECR 1629; Case 190/87 *Moormann* [1988] ECR 4689; Case C-83/92 *Pierrel* [1993] ECR I-6419.

which public authorities shall have the competence to take action in the event of violation of the rules by private parties. This is the second issue – the distribution of competence between home and host States with regard to *enforcement* of the Community rules.

Many of these tensions can be identified in the 're-regulatory bargain' found in the e-commerce Directive, Directive 2000/31. Perhaps most of all one may observe how the complex map of accumulated regulatory endeavour in the Member States is not readily reduced to a simple, single regime for the conduct of an integrated market in services supplied by electronic means.[21] But the dominant concern of the Directive is to introduce a principle of home State control as a basis for an integrated European e-commerce market.

4 E-COMMERCE AND HARMONISATION

Article 1(1) of Directive 2000/31 explains that the measure 'seeks to contribute to the proper functioning of the internal market by ensuring the free movement of information society services between the Member States'. It approximates, to the extent necessary for the achievement of this objective, 'certain national provisions on information society services relating to the internal market, the establishment of service providers, commercial communications, electronic contracts, the liability of intermediaries, codes of conduct, out-of-court dispute settlements, court actions and co-operation between Member States'. This is Article 1(2), and in principle it describes at a general level the field occupied by the Directive.

Article 1(6) provides that this Directive 'does not affect measures taken at Community or national level, in the respect of Community law, in order to promote cultural and linguistic diversity and to ensure the defence of pluralism'. This appears to carve out a permissible area of host State intervention that is not excluded by the Directive. However, plainly intervention motivated by these concerns would require justification according to standards recognised by the Court under primary Community law in so far as it impeded the free movement of goods or services.[22] It is more broadly plain from Article 1(5) that this Directive does not govern the whole sweep of regulatory issues that arise in the e-commerce sector. This sub-

---

21 For an overview, looking beyond the Directive, see M. De Cock Buning, E. Hondius, C. Prins & M. De Vries, 'Consumer@Protection. EU: an analysis of European Consumer Legislation in the Information Society', 24 *Journal of Consumer Policy* 287 (2001); I. Walden, 'Regulating electronic commerce: Europe in the global E-conomy', 26 ELRev. 529 (2001). The Commission has tried to pull together relevant information at <www.europa.eu.int/information_society/topics/telecoms/index_en.htm>.

22 On the compatibility of national rules governing use of language with Article 28 EC, see Case C-369/89 *Piageme* v. *Peeters* [1991] ECR I-2971, which provoked a Commission Communication on the issue, COM (93) 532, OJ 1993 C345/3; Case C-85/94 *Piageme* v. *Peeters* [1995] ECR I-2955; Case C-385/96 *Goerres* [1998] ECR I-4431; Case C-33/97 *Colim* v. *Bigg's Continent Noord* [1999] ECR I-3175. Case C-366/98 *Geffroy* judgment of 12 September 2000. For criticism of the Court's perceived lack of respect for local diversity, see A. Fenet, 'Diversité linguistique et construction européenne', 37 RTDE 235 (2001); C. Boch, 'Language Protection and Free Trade: the Triumph of the Homo McDonaldus', 4 *Euro Public Law* 379 (1998).

paragraph excludes a number of important areas from the Directive's application, including taxation. EC regulation of e-commerce involves a complicated intermingling of national and Community rules, and Directive 2000/31 is just one component.

4.1 The substance

Article 3(1) of the Directive provides that 'Each Member State shall ensure that the information society services provided by a service provider established on its territory comply with the national provisions applicable in the Member State in question which fall within the coordinated field'. The notion of the 'co-ordinated field' is explained in Article 2; it covers, in short, requirements imposed on a service provider in respect of taking up and pursuit of activity in the e-commerce field, as defined by the Directive.[23] This, then, constitutes the obligation imposed on the home State. It must supervise compliance with the rules by operators established on its territory. Article 3(2) provides that 'Member States may not, for reasons falling within the co-ordinated field, restrict the freedom to provide information society services from another Member State.' This is the corollary; it is the host State's responsibility to allow access to its market for services emanating from another Member State. For matters falling within the field covered by the Directive, the home State shall secure compliance with the relevant rules and the host State must not exercise powers to exclude services for reasons falling within the occupied field.[24] The situation prevailing prior to the Directive provided that the market remained fragmented along national lines in so far as home States applied one set of rules and host States applied different rules which may be justified according to the Court's case law despite their restrictive effect on cross-border trade or which may even survive, and hinder trade, simply because of the size and cost of the task confronting traders wishing to challenge even plainly unlawful technical rules. Under the regime introduced by the Directive, this pattern is adjusted so that common rules, agreed at Community level, govern the sector (within the Directive's scope). The home State secures observance of the rules; the host State may not demand conformity with stricter or even different rules. Home State control is thus strongly emphasised.

The obligations to be imposed on service providers under Directive 2000/31 are found in Chapter II, comprising Articles 4 to 15 of the Directive. Article 5 covers general information to be provided, and contains transparency requirements. Member States are directed to ensure that particular pieces of information shall be rendered by the service provider easily, directly and in permanently accessible form to the recipients of the service and competent authorities. This obligation covers the name of the service provider, the address at which the service provider is established, and de-

23 Recital 21 provides examples of matters that fall outside the co-ordinated field; 'Member States' legal requirements relating to goods such as safety standards, labelling obligations, or liability for goods, or Member States' requirements relating to the delivery or the transport of goods'.

24 Article 3(3) excludes fields referred to in the Directive's Annex from the application of these two paragraphs.

tails, including an e-mail address, which allow the provider to be contacted rapidly and communicated with in a direct and effective manner. Moreover, where the service provider is registered in a trade or similar public register, the relevant information shall be communicated; so, too, where the activity is subject to an authorisation scheme; and accompanying rules in Article 5(1)(f) also require disclosure of relevant information in the case of the regulated professions, which cover those falling within the Community's measures governing recognition of professional qualifications under either Article 1(d) of Directive 89/48 or Article 1(f) of Directive 92/51.[25] Article 5(2) of Directive 2000/31 further provides that Member States are to require that where references are made to price, 'these are to be indicated clearly and unambiguously and, in particular, must indicate whether they are inclusive of tax and delivery costs'.

There is no value in simply repeating in this contribution what is set out already in the Directive. I simply summarise the remaining provisions of the Directive which deal with regulatory obligations to be imposed by Member States on e-traders. Article 6 of the Directive concerns commercial communications, and adds further rules governing information to be provided, in particular the requirement that the commercial communication shall be clearly identifiable as such. Article 7 deals with unsolicited commercial communications. It is provided that Member States which permit such activity by e-mail shall ensure that such commercial communications sent by traders based on their territory shall be identifiable clearly and unambiguously on receipt, and that they shall take measures to ensure such traders consult regularly and respect registers in which parties have chosen to opt out from receipt of such unsolicited electronic approaches. Recital 30 in the Directive's lengthy Preamble states that in States that permit unsolicited commercial e-communications, 'the setting up of appropriate industry filtering initiatives should be encouraged and facilitated'. So the Directive does not rule out unsolicited commercial communications – that is a choice resting with the Member States – but it imposes regulation on such practices. Article 8 deals with the particular issue of the regulated professions.

Articles 9 to 11 deal with contracts concluded by electronic means. Article 9 requires Member States to ensure that their legal system allows contracts to be concluded by electronic means. This represents an updating of the law that is plainly essential to meet the demands of technological change. Article 10 governs information to be provided in the case of contracts concluded by electronic means and Article 11 concerns the placing of the order. Articles 12 to 15 of the Directive regulate the liability of intermediary service providers.

This, then, is the basic content of the 're-regulatory' regime agreed at Community level. These requirements constitute the agreed regime for e-commerce in the Community. They represent the practical reality that harmonisation involves not only the establishment of a common framework for trade, but also some choices about what types of conduct should be permitted, and on what terms. The thrust of the Community's intervention is in favour of transparency – that the consumer should be more fully informed of the nature of the transaction than would neces-

25 Article 2(g) of Directive 2000/31.

sarily occur in an unregulated market. Such legal requirements of information disclosure may be analysed as appropriate to encourage consumers to participate more actively and confidently in this sector than they otherwise would, in the absence of a guaranteed floor of legal protection. It may also be considered that such rules protect the interests of scrupulous traders who, in the absence of regulation, would find their honest practices undermined by the actions of rogues. Information disclosure has a healthy pedigree as a form of legal correction of market failures, and it has been widely practised by the Community in the past. Many of the Directives that harmonise laws governing protection of the economic interests of consumers adopt as their principal regulatory technique the mandatory disclosure of information by traders to consumers.[26]

4.2 *Enforcement*

As explained above, the structure of the Directive provides that the home State secures observance of the rules and that it is not open to the host State to demand conformity with stricter or even different rules. This is a model driven strongly by the desire to integrate markets (albeit according to standards of regulation established at Community level). Traders need not worry that different jurisdictions will present different regulatory demands (within the scope of the Directive). But this powerful emphasis on home State control possesses a further dimension. Where a violation of the rules is committed, the competence of the host State to take action is closely confined. It is the home State that is allocated the primary role in remedying infractions of the rules agreed in the Directive. So here, too, home State control is the principal component of the Community's regulatory strategy.

In principle, host States may not, for reasons falling within the co-ordinated field, restrict the freedom to provide information society services emanating from another Member State. This is the basic integrative rule established by Article 3(2) of Directive 2000/31. Exceptionally, however, it is provided in Article 3(4) of the Directive that a host State may restrict the freedom to provide information society services from another Member State provided specified conditions are satisfied. These embrace both substantive requirements and procedural requirements, which in both respects raise a high threshold that must be crossed before a host State is entitled to respond to breach of the rules by impeding market access. So a restriction may be imposed only provided the measures are necessary for one of a list of defined

26 E.g. Directive 85/577 to protect the consumer in respect of contracts negotiated away from business premises, OJ 1985 L372/31, Directive 90/314 on package travel, package holidays and package tours, OJ 1990 L158/59, Directive 87/102 for the approximation of the laws, regulations and administrative provision of the Member States concerning consumer credit, OJ L 42/48 (as amended by Directive 90/88 OJ 1990 L61/14). Even measures that go so far as to prohibit particular practices also include thematic emphasis on the value of transparency, see e.g. Articles 4(2), 5 of Directive 93/13 on unfair terms in consumer contracts, OJ 1993 L95/29. See generally S. Grundmann, W. Kerber & S. Weatherill (eds.), *Party Autonomy and the role of Information in the Internal Market* (Berlin: de Gruyter, 2001).

reasons, embracing public policy,[27] the protection of public health, public security, including the safeguarding of national security and defence, and the protection of consumers, including investors, and, moreover, the measures in question must be taken against a service 'which prejudices one of these objectives or which presents a serious and grave risk of prejudice to those objectives', and which is proportionate to those objectives. But even where a situation arises in which these high hurdles are crossed, the host State may take action to restrict the service only provided it has already asked the home State to act, and it has not acted or has not taken adequate action, and provided it has notified both the Commission and the home State of its intention to adopt restrictive measures. An emergency procedure is available in Article 3(5), which allows the procedural – but not the substantive – pre-conditions to be dispensed with by the host State 'in the case of urgency', but the overall purpose and effect of this structure is plainly to permit host States to interfere with cross-border trade only in very exceptional, extreme circumstances. The key to securing an integrated market in e-commerce is to establish rules at Community level but then to place a heavy emphasis on home State application of the rules as the normal rule. Presumably any other circumstances, beyond those envisaged in Article 3(4) of the Directive, in which a host State is faced by service providers who are guilty of misapplication of the rules must be addressed by remedial means which do not involve a denial of access by the service provider to the host State's market. This will doubtless involve approaches made by the host State to the home State, and ultimately, should legal action be required because of default by the authorities in the home State in supervising traders based on their territory, this might involve action by the Commission pursuant to Article 226 EC, by the Member State itself pursuant to Article 227 EC, and/ or by action before national courts relying on the direct effect of Community law.

The Directive also envisages in Articles 16 and 17 respectively supplementary implementation by codes of conduct and out-of-court dispute settlement as well as specifying judicial remedies under Article 18 and sanctions under Article 20, while also envisaging co-operation in enforcement in Article 19. But the impetus towards the integration of markets is strongly emphasised by the almost total surrender of host State competence to retaliate against breach of the agreed Community rules by closing off its market to infringing services.[28]

27 'In particular the prevention, investigation, detection and prosecution of criminal offences, including the protection of minors and the fight against any incitement to hatred on grounds of race, sex, religion and nationality, and violations of human dignity concerning individual persons'.

28 See similarly the 'Television without Frontiers' Directive, Directive 89/552, OJ 1989 L298, amended by Dir. 97/36, OJ 1997 L202, examined in this vein by the current author in S. Weatherill, 'Pre-Emption, Harmonisation and the Distribution of Competence to Regulate the Internal Market' in: C. Barnard and J. Scott (eds.), *The Law of the Single European Market: Unpacking the Premises* (2002), ch. 2.

5 THE CONSTITUTIONAL DIMENSION

I have suggested above that EC trade law under the Treaty may be analysed as a device for indirectly feeding otherwise unrepresented but affected interests into the political process of producing regulation at national level. So *Cassis de Dijon* subverts host State autonomy and demands justification for trade-restrictive rules that reflects their impact in the context of an integrating, inter-State market. In this vein, one way of interpreting primary Community law governing free movement, as shaped by the Court in and since *Cassis de Dijon*, is that it is built on the assumption that the simple fact that national laws have been 'validated' by adoption (at some time in the past) according to the recognised political process in the State concerned is not enough to justify its continued application. EC trade law demands more; it demands a justification in the light of the damage such a rule may exert on the building of a cross-border market. This is central to the EC's modus operandi. It pursues the construction of a European market, but it does not pursue the construction of a European State. Instead, it assumes the continuing political existence of the Member States. But it subjects the exercise of power by the Member States to a control that is designed to restrain them from inflicting unjustified harm on the market-building process. *Cassis de Dijon* represents a classic illustration. The rule at stake in that decision protected the interests of German producers. But it did not serve the interests of German consumers, who were robbed of wider choice. Nor did it assist traders based in other Member States who were, in practice, excluded from competing in the German market by the rigid rule of product composition. In fact, the German rule illustrated how market regulation generated by national political processes may be inapt to capture and represent the interests at stake once markets have evolved beyond the territorial limits of a single State. So, in this sense, EC trade law bridges the gap between the quest to create a European market and the admission that such a process does not and cannot wholly dismantle State power in Europe and does not and cannot involve a wholesale transfer of decision-making competence to European level. Instead, State power is controlled and, among other things, prevented from imposing external costs by policies of economic protectionism.

From this perspective, the free movement case law 'forces' host States to justify their choices in the light of the impact on affected constituencies who are not otherwise (adequately) represented in domestic local political processes. The *Cassis de Dijon* principle, elaborated by the Court, achieves a form of correction of local political processes that are not attuned to the broader sweep of market integration in Europe. And a very similar message may be gleaned from the law governing the enforcement by home States of 're-regulatory' standards once they have been adopted under Community secondary legislation. Here too EC trade law changes the orthodox expectation of the identity of the parties to whom national law-makers and law-enforcers are responsible. European markets induce wider horizons for national officials.

Under the 're-regulatory bargain', interests that over time have prompted regulation of the market in host States have not been swept aside (though this may occur); rather, the fact that their expression collided with the process of European market building has caused them to be absorbed into the EC legal order and it is now necessary to look (albeit not necessarily exclusively) to Community level – the Directive – for the location of the rule which reflects protection of those interests. This then plays out in the context of a trader in home State X supplying consumers in host State Y. Then, interested parties in the host State no longer expect enforcement by 'their' authorities; rather the home State, implementing the Directive under the model of 'indirect rule' foreseen by Articles 10 and 249 EC, is responsible. So the home State X has, via EC law's 're-regulation', become obliged to work as a law enforcement agency on behalf of consumers in host State Y. This is made explicit in recital 22 to Directive 2000/31, where the home State is stated to be acting on behalf of 'not only the citizens of its own country but for all Community citizens'.

The immediate question, of course, is just *why* home State officials would act in this way. True, home State control is efficient, for the home State is closest to the trader and best able to act if the rules are violated. And home State control is undeniably conducive to driving forward market integration. However, especially (but not only) where the traders based in the home State are politically influential and where damage done by failure to police compliance with EC Directives would largely be felt by consumers in host States, it is not obvious that there are incentives for home States to act effectively to enforce the 're-regulatory bargain'. Quite the reverse – the domestic political mandate is not tied to the interests of out-of-State consumers. The EC intervention is based on the construction of a European market but associated rule-enforcement is tied to the reality of State systems which are apt to generate decisions (about law enforcement as well as law making) that reflect the interests able directly to influence State political processes; and those are narrower than those envisaged at EC level as affected by market-building achieved by the adoption of secondary legislation. This is the dark side of the picture, painted in its brighter version above, that reserves to national bodies primary competence for administering EC law in preference to establishing a large European bureaucracy. States may cheat.[29] There are tempting strategies for 'creative compliance', such as calculated shrinking budgets allocated to enforcement of EC-derived rules, which may be lawful and may be unlawful under the 'spongy' standard of effective enforcement,[30] but will in neither case be readily tracked by the Commission, given the constitutional and resource constraints that impede its ability to inquire into practice 'on the ground' in the Member States. It is significant in this regard that the Commission's 'League Ta-

---

29 On the breadth of reasons for non-compliance, see P. Van den Bossche, 'In search of remedies for non-compliance: the Experience of the EC', 3 MJ 371 (1996). Of course there is also plenty of evidence of how EC rules are absorbed and taken seriously by local agencies; e.g. T. Daintith (ed.), *Implementing EC Law in the UK: Structures for Indirect Rule* (Wiley, 1995); J. Vervaele (ed.), *Administrative Law Application and Enforcement of Community Law in the Netherlands* (Kluwer, 1994); J. Vervaele et al. (eds.), *Compliance and Enforcement of EC Law* (Kluwer, 1999). For the case that relatively little statistical evidence supports the view that compliance with EC law is poor, see T. Boerzel, 'Non-compliance in the EU: pathology or statistical artefact?', 8 JEPP 803 (2001).

30 When, for example, does allocation of a small budget to an enforcement agency breach Articles 10 and 249 EC rather than merely reflect fiscal prudence in the allocation of scarce public resources? Many matters of detail are left unaddressed by the Court's general statement that enforcement of EC rules in the Member States must be 'effective' (see e.g. Case C-213/99 *De Andrade* judgment of 7 December 2000).

bles',[31] which are designed to shame defaulting Member States into better compliance with their obligations under adopted Directives, in fact record only transposition on paper. They reveal nothing about the depth of penetration of the rules into national administrative and judicial culture. So, at least in some circumstances, home States have incentives to take a soft approach to their obligations of enforcement. Moreover, as explained above, host States are severely limited under the Directive in their capacity to retaliate to misapplication of the rules by closing off market access (which, in the e-commerce sector, might anyway be technologically difficult).

Much of this is, of course, equally applicable to primary law. States have incentives to evade their obligations to adhere to the rules of free movement, particularly where domestic suppliers agitate for protection because they fear they will be slaughtered by cross-border competition. The control mechanism that has dominated the development of EC law is litigation. This can illuminatingly be analysed as EC law's method for ensuring that national actors charged with the legal responsibility to apply EC law in favour of affected parties beyond those dominant nationally do not shirk their task as a result of pressures consequent on their location within national political milieux and their absence of direct political accountability to 'European market interests'. EC law's deep penetration into national systems is properly regarded as the principal feature which distinguishes it from orthodox international law. EC law has teeth and their incisive effect renders credible the commitments undertaken on a reciprocal basis by all the Member States. In connection with the Treaty rules on free movement, litigation driven by interested economic actors has played a vigorous role in securing adaptation of national regulatory cultures. So, equally at the level of secondary legislation, we might assume that violation of the re-regulatory bargain by a home State, whether deliberate or not, will be the subject of a litigious response that will re-direct defaulting national practice back to the European straight and narrow.

That may happen. But, as I have argued more fully elsewhere,[32] there are reasons to be cautious about the value of litigation generally in securing the stabilisation of the internal market; and, in particular, there are reasons to be anxious that the likelihood of litigation serving to restrain violation of the obligation to regulate markets effectively in accordance with Community Directives is much lower than the likelihood of litigation aimed at opening up markets in line with the Treaty provisions governing free movement. Litigation as a strategy is important, but its contribution to fostering reliable adherence to the rules of EC law is likely to be ad hoc and ex post facto. In particular, litigation is more likely to play a prominent role in securing the enforcement of the law of free movement, where violations are relatively clear-cut, tend to hurt identifiable individual traders and concern affected parties commercially enthusiastic to pursue their complaint, than it is in the context of the enforcement

31 Available via <www.europa.eu.int>.

32 S. Weatherill, 'Reflections on EC law's 'implementation imbalance' in the light of the ruling in Hedley Lomas' in: L. Krämer, H.-W. Micklitz and K. Tonner (eds.), *Law and Diffuse Interests in the European Legal Order* (VIEW/ Nomos, 1997); S. Weatherill, 'Addressing problems of Imbalanced Implementation in EC Law: Remedies in an Institutional Perspective', in: C Kilpatrick, T. Novitz and P. Skidmore (eds.), *The Future of Remedies in Europe* (Hart, 2000).

of the 're-regulatory' bargain, where harm is inflicted on diffuse interests – consumers, proponents of environmental protection – and individual litigants are unlikely to possess a sufficient incentive to pursue the defaulting State, and may not even possess a 'right' recognised by law. This is EC law's 'implementation imbalance'. In any legal order, the orthodox theoretical assumption in such circumstances would be that collective action would be required. The Commission plays this role in the Community system under Article 226 EC, but its resources are limited and its intervention is typically slow and on occasion disrupted by politicking. Some national systems may permit or promote collective intervention, but this varies State by State and Community rules are largely lacking [33]. In summary, litigation can be no more than a single component of a more broadly-based strategy for securing a viable internal market.

The Commission is perfectly well aware of this. It continues to rest a heavy emphasis on litigation as a tool of market management but it has wisely concluded that it must develop more pervasive methods for stabilising the internal market than the essentially ad hoc, ex post facto route taken by it and by private litigants through the courts. In summary,[34] the Commission has busily aimed to devise a web of arrangements designed to improve and intensify co-operation in the management of the internal market, both vertically, between itself and interested public and private parties in the Member States, and horizontally, between different actors at national level. This strategy embraces obligations to notify the Commission of national initiatives that may interfere with cross-border trade, thereby to facilitate Commission supervision, exhortation to States to publicise contact addresses at which dissatisfaction with practice may be directed and frequent soft law encouragement to improve the quality of national supervision and sanctions. A recent example of the Commission's strenuous attempts to nurture cross-border administrative co-operation that is designed to improve the management of the internal market without the need to rely on litigation is provided by SOLVIT, the Internal Market Problem Solving Network.[35] The Commission also hopes that periodic publication of 'League Tables' and 'Scoreboards' will induce better rates of compliance without the need for more formal approaches to defaulting States. Techniques devoted to improving transparency in the management of the market are fundamentally aimed at generating *confidence* in the viability of the internal market among both traders and consumers.[36] The Commission deserves credit for seeking imaginative schemes for improving compliance with EC law in a political environment which firmly locks it into the model which places primary emphasis on State bodies as those responsible for application of the rules 'on the ground'. The inclusion of an insistence on improving the application of

---

33 For a small step that may nevertheless have relevance in the e-commerce sector see the Consumer Injunctions Directive, Dir. 98/27 OJ 1998 L166/51.

34 For more detail see K. Mortelmans, 'The Common Market, the Internal Market and the single market, What's in a Market?',35 CMLRev 101 (1998); S. Weatherill, 'New Strategies for Managing the EC's Internal Market', in: M. Freeman (ed.), *Current Legal Problems* (Oxford, Oxford University Press, Vol 53, 2000); K. Armstrong, 'Governance and the Single European Market' in: P. Craig & G. De Burca (eds.), *The Evolution of EU Law* (OUP, 1999).

35 OJ 2001 L331/79.

36 E.g. Commission report on the Consumer Action Plan, COM (01) 486, esp. p. 11.

EC rules at national level in the Commission's White Paper on Governance, published in the summer of 2001, confirms that this is no mere technical matter.[37] It goes to the heart of sustaining a viable system for governing the Union built on horizontal and vertical co-operation between actors at different levels rather than on any desire to make a State at European level.

6 Conclusion

This contribution has explored the prominence of 'home State control' as the basis for the creation and management of the internal market, with particular reference to the e-commerce sector. Primary EC law contains a preference for home State control in the sense that a host State is entitled to apply its local rules in a manner that obstructs trade originating in other Member States only provided it is able to demonstrate a sufficiently strong justification for those rules – a 'mandatory requirement' or, more generally, a reason of sufficient weight serving the public interest. The pattern of 'home State control' is taken over into secondary legislation, Directive 2000/31. This requires the e-trader's home State to enforce defined standards of good conduct, relating to, for example, the provision of information to consumers, and, in return, the host State is required to allow e-traders to operate in its market without subjection to further requirements imposed within the field co-ordinated by the Directive. This permits e-traders to plan an integrated commercial strategy for the whole of the EU market, confident in the expectation that the common legal regime introduced for the EU by Directive 2000/31 will preclude any need to devise separate approaches State-by-State. The emphasis on home State control as the key to an integrated market is buttressed by rules dealing with the consequences should there be breach of the regulatory standards mandated by the Directive. Only in exceptional circumstances may a host State respond to violation of these standards by denying an e-trader access to its market. In principle it is normally for the home State to rectify the problem.

Directive 2000/31 represents an interesting example of the constitutional implications of the building of an internal market in the European Union under a system which assumes the dominance of national legal and administrative institutions in the implementation and enforcement of rules agreed at transnational level. Community law operates by injecting into national practice an obligation to respect interests in the making of a transnational economy. The daring attempt to make a European market without investing any significant resources in the creation of European-level enforcement agencies is opposed by basic principles of representative democracy which remain rooted at State level. State actors have been placed in a context in which they are expected to address and promote the interests of parties with no access or only limited access to national political processes. As explained in this contribution, this is true under the Treaty rules governing free movement and it is true under the relevant instruments of secondary legislation. The inefficiencies and

37 COM (01) 428 p. 25-26. Similarly, Green Paper on EU Consumer Protection, COM (01) 531, p. 16-19, endorsed by the Economic and Social Committee, OJ 2002 C125/1.

inequities that flow from the exercise of State regulatory autonomy are addressed under the home State/ host State model which has been used imaginatively to achieve a vertical and horizontal redistribution of competence to exercise public functions in order to promote the achievement of the EC's objectives. In this sense membership of the European Union and subjection to its law generates an adaptation of national legal and political orders which reflects the reality of the impact of transnational economic, political and social activity, though there is no assumption of the need for a new State at European level. Competence distribution between home and host States is central to understanding the techniques used both under the Treaty and under secondary legislation to pursue the quest to minimise inefficient dual regulation in the European market. For e-commerce, more than most sectors, it will be intriguing to observe whether the law is able to meet the expectations of technological change.

Electronic signatures: A survey of the directive and the legislation in the United Kingdom and the Netherlands

Rob van Esch

1 INTRODUCTION

In the information society a growing number of legal acts are performed electronically. For example contracts concluded over the Internet are becoming more commonplace. As the value of such transactions, especially in a business-consumer relationship, is usually very small, parties in many electronic transactions refrain from using electronic signatures as a means to verify the identity of the other party. In that case the supplier of goods or services knowingly accepts the risk that the other party is not who he says he is. The customer accepts a similar risk. The general expectancy is that in the future the value of electronic transactions will increase as a result of the growing confidence of enterprises and consumers in electronic commerce. This will lead to a growing need for electronic signatures that can perform the same functions as a hand-written signature.

There is no point in using electronic signatures in electronic commerce if the applicable law does not recognise electronic signatures. By recognition I mean that the law attributes some legal effect to electronic signatures, for example by accepting electronic signatures as evidence in legal proceedings or by accepting an electronic signature as a substitute for a hand-written signature with respect to statutory requirements of form. In the past most legal systems did not provide any certainty with regard to the legal status of electronic signatures. With the rise of electronic commerce lawyers and (national and supranational) legislators sensed the urgency for a legal framework for electronic signatures to support the development of electronic commerce. One of the first organisations that recognised the need for a legal framework for electronic commerce in general and electronic signatures in particular was the United Nations Commission on International Trade Law (UNCITRAL). This organisation published a Model Law on Electronic Commerce in 1996.[1] This Model Law contains a provision regarding electronic signatures in article 7. In short this provision puts the electronic signature on a par with hand-written signatures if the electronic signature is based on a reliable method and fulfils the identification function

1 The UNCITRAL Model Law on Electronic Commerce with Guide to Enactment 1996 with additional article 5 *bis* as adopted in 1998, New York: United Nations 1999.

H. Snijders, S. Weatherill (eds.), *E-commerce Law*, 27-48

and the approval function of a hand-written signature.[2] During the process of drafting the UNCITRAL Model Law on Electronic Commerce and afterwards many national legislators have enacted their own legislation regarding electronic signatures. In the United States Utah was the first state to adopt an act on electronic signatures. It enacted the Utah Digital Signature Act in 1995.[3] Many US states followed the example of Utah. In 2000 a federal law, the Electronic Signatures in Global and National Commerce Act (the E-sign Act 2000), came into force, which provides in section 101 that a signature may not be denied legal effect solely because it is in electronic form and a contract may not be denied legal effect, validity or enforceability, because an electronic signature was used in its formation. In other countries outside the US similar developments were and are taking place.[4] Many of those national statutes are based on the principle of the functional equivalent as laid down in the UNCITRAL Model Law on Electronic Commerce 1996.

2 The European Directive on Electronic Signatures

In the European Union some Member States enacted statutes regarding electronic signatures. Take, for example, the German Signaturgesetz 1997 which was incorporated into article 3 of the Informations- und Kommunikationsdienste Gesetz. This German act created a legal framework for Trusted Third Parties providing certification services for digital signatures.[5] Another example is the Italian Electronic Document and Digital Signature Act 1997 (Legge Bassanini, 59/1997 Act), which contains provisions in article 10 regarding the legal status of a digital signature.[6]

These initiatives of some Member States were not warmly welcomed by the European Commission. In its communication to the European Parliament, the Council, the Economic and Social Committee and the Committee of the Regions entitled '*Ensuring Security and Trust in Electronic Communication. Towards a European Framework for Digital Signatures and Encryption*', the Commission wrote that the very divergent legal and technical approaches which have already appeared and the absence of any legal environment in other Member States -also possibly justified- might constitute a serious barrier to doing business and communicating throughout the European Union.[7] The Commission felt that a common framework at Community level was ur-

---

2 In 2001 the UNCITRAL adopted the Model Law on Electronic Signatures. This Model Law provides additional legal certainty regarding the use of electronic signatures building on the flexible principle contained in article 7 of the Model Law on Electronic Commerce 1996. The Model Law on Electronic Commerce and the Model Law on Electronic Signatures are accessible on the website of the UNCITRAL www.uncitral.org.

3 This act was published in The *EDI Law Review* 1995/3, p. 157-196

4 For example the Singaporean Electronic Transactions Act 1998.

5 The English translation was published in The *EDI Law Review* 1997/3, p. 205-227.

6 See for a brief commentary on this act P. Palmerini, *Italy*, The *EDI Law Review* 1997/4, p. 281-288.

7 Communication from the Commission of the European Parliament, the Council, the Economic and Social Committee and the Committee of the Regions, COM (97) 503, p. 15-16.

gently needed and should be put in place at the latest by the year 2000. Subsequently the Commission on 16 June 1998 submitted a Proposal for a European Parliament and Council Directive on a common framework for electronic signatures.[8] This proposal resulted in Directive 1999/93/EC of the European Parliament and of the Council of 13 December 1999 on a Community framework for electronic signatures.[9] This Directive should have been implemented by the Member States on 19 July 2001.

In the United Kingdom the Directive was implemented by the adoption on 25 May 2000 of the Electronic Communications Act 2000, hereinafter referred to as the ECA.

In the Netherlands a bill was presented to parliament on 18 May 2001, hereinafter referred to as the DESA (Dutch Electronic Signatures Act).[10] This bill has not yet been passed.

Hereafter I will first give some examples of electronic signatures and will describe their underlying technologies. Then I will give an outline of the most relevant provisions of the European Directive on electronic signatures followed by a comparative analysis of the implementation of these provisions in the ECA and the DESA.[11]

3 ELECTRONIC SIGNATURES

3.1 Examples of electronic signatures

Article 2.1 of the Directive defines electronic signature as data in electronic form which is attached to or logically associated with other electronic data and which serves as a method of authentication. This definition is generic and encompasses all kinds of technologies that can be used to establish the authenticity of an electronic message.

Usually an electronic signature fulfils at least two functions of the hand-written signature:

(1) the recipient of signed (electronic) data can verify the identity of the sender by means of the signature (identification function);
(2) by signing the data the sender expresses his will to be bound by the declaration contained in the signed data (approval function).

---

8 Official Journal of the European Communities 1998, C 325/5.

9 OJ 2000, L 13/12.

10 The specifications of this Act are 'Aanpassing van Boek 3 en Boek 6 van het Burgerlijk Wetboek, de Telecommunicatiewet en de Wet op de economische delicten inzake elektronische handtekeningen ter uitvoering van richtlijn nr. 1999/93/EG van het Europees Parlement en de Raad van de Europese Unie van 13 december 1999 betreffende een gemeenschappelijk kader voor elektronische handtekeningen (PbEG L 13) (Wet elektronische handtekeningen), *Kamerstukken II* 2000/01, 27 743, nr. 1'.

11 See J. Dumortier, 'Directive 1999/93/EC on a Community framework for electronic signatures', in: A.R. Lodder & H.W.K. Kaspersen, *eDirectives. Guide to European Union Law on E-commerce* (The Hague: Kluwer Law International 2002), p. 33-65.

For an overview of possible other functions of the electronic signature I refer to the Guide to Enactment of the UNCITRAL Model Law on Electronic Commerce 1996.[12]

In payment systems PIN codes are being used to verify the identity of the client. The reliability of this means of identification depends on the customer maintaining the confidentiality of the PIN codes. One can argue whether the PIN codes used in payment systems fulfil the approval function of the electronic signature.

Another method of authentication requires a person to write down a signature with a special pen on a special tablet. This system registers the characteristics of the signing process like the form of the signature, the pressure on the pen, the speed with which the signature is drawn etc, and compares those data with data about the signature of the signer previously stored by the recipient of the electronic message. The reliability of this method depends on the adopted False Rejection Rate and the complementary False Acceptance Rate. These rates are being used by the recipient of electronic messages because a hundred percent similarity between the received data and the stored data is unrealistic. For one, the form of a signature of a certain person will never be the same. The lower the False Rejection Rate the lower the chance will be that a customer will incorrectly not be recognised by the system. On the other hand, in that case the chance will be higher that a person acting fraudulently will be recognised as the customer (the so-called False Acceptance Rate).

Several methods have been developed based on biometrics. These methods enable the recipient of an electronic message to verify the identity of the originator by comparing data regarding certain physical characteristics of that person with the data regarding that person's characteristics previously stored by the recipient. Examples of such methods are fingerprint or voice recognition. The reliability of such methods depends to a great extent on the amount of data that will be used for the comparison. If for example a fingerprint is only scanned at and compared with fifty points of the finger the comparison is much more unreliable than in case the scan and comparison involve a thousand points. Furthermore, here also the reliability depends on the False Acceptance Rate used. As a person may have dirt on his finger, for example, or a cold which affects his voice, a zero False Acceptance Rate would result in an unacceptable number of customers being rejected incorrectly (the so-called False Rejection Rate). On the other hand, the lower the False Acceptance Rate the higher the chance that the finger or the voice of a person acting fraudulently will be recognised as the finger or the voice of a customer.

Although the Directive has a generic scope and covers all electronic signatures that fall within the definition of electronic signatures in article 2 of the Directive, the main part of its provisions focuses on the digital signature and certification service providers. A digital signature is based on encryption technology. The digital signing process works as follows: the software of the sender of an electronic message cal-

12 See note 1, p. 38.

culates the hash value of the electronic message by performing certain compressing functions. This hash value is uniquely linked with the message. If one bit in the message is changed the calculated hash value no longer belongs to that message. After having calculated the hash value the software encrypts the hash value with the secret private key of the sender on the basis of an algorithm. This encrypted hash value is the digital signature. The recipient decrypts the encrypted hash value with the public key of the sender, calculates the hash value belonging to the received message himself and compares the decrypted hash value with the calculated hash value. If these two hash values are the same he knows that the message was digitally signed by someone who had the private key of the purported sender in his possession and he knows that the integrity of the message itself has not been tampered with.

Below you will find two charts giving a visual impression of the process of digitally signing an electronic message and the process of verifying the digital signature.

One question remains to be answered: how does the recipient know for sure that the public key with which he verifies the digital signature is the public key belonging to the signer? This certainty is created by the Trusted Third Party (TTP) also called the certification service provider (CSP). After having generated the key pair consisting of a secret private key and a complementary public key, the holder of the public key will request the CSP to issue a certificate. For this purpose the holder must present the public key to the CSP and must identify himself, for example by means of a passport. The CSP will then issue an electronic certificate to the holder confirming that the public key belongs to that person. This certificate is digitally signed by the CSP. The holder can send a copy of this certificate together with the electronic message and the digital signature to the recipient of the electronic message.

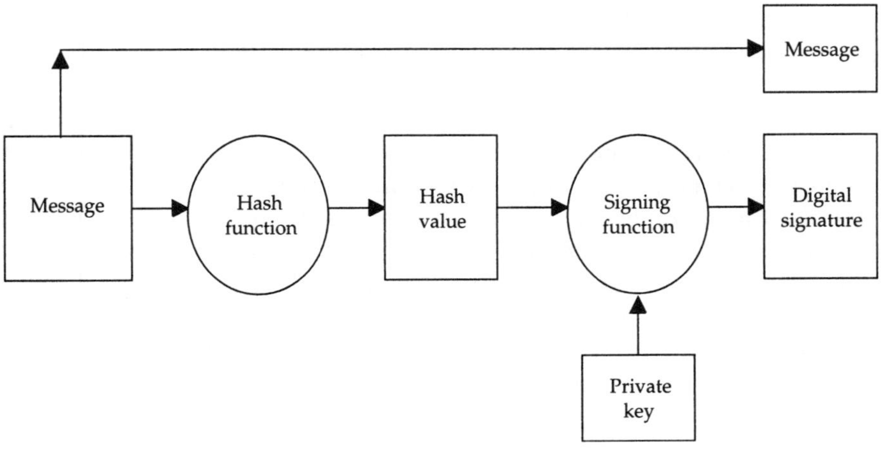

Figure 1: The process of signing on the sender's side

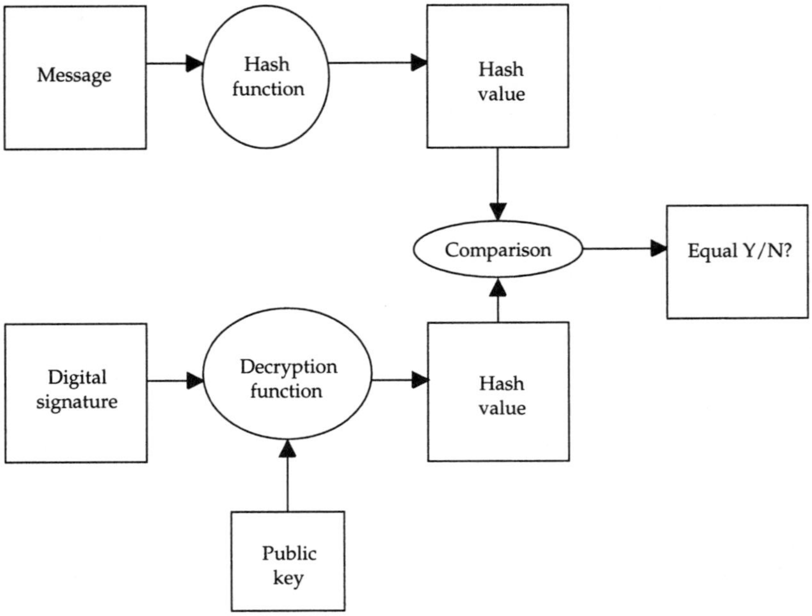

Figure 2: The verification process on the recipient's side

3.2 *Terminology of the Directive*

Although article 2 of the Directive starts with a generic definition of the concept of 'electronic signature' nearly all the other definitions of article 2 are related to digital signatures as described in the previous paragraph.

The Directive distinguishes between qualified certificates and other certificates. Qualified certificates are certificates that meet the requirements of Annex I of the Directive and are issued by a CSP that meets the requirements of Annex II of the Directive.

For the creation of a digital signature the signatory needs software, including, among others, the encryption software with the algorithm used to encrypt the hash value. Furthermore the secret private key needs to be stored somewhere. It can be stored on the hard disk of the computer of the signatory but in many systems the private key is stored on a chip card. The reason for this is that a hard disk could be visited by a hacker who might be able to get access to the private key. In article 2 of the Directive the private key is called ' signature-creation data'. The software and the chip card are called 'signature-creation device'. A 'secure-signature-creation device' means a signature-creation device that meets the requirements laid down in Annex III of the Directive.

The recipient needs software and the public key of the sender to verify the digital signature of the sender. In article 2 of the Directive the public key is called 'signature-verification-data'.

The software is called 'signature-verification device'.

4 Scope of the Directive

4.1 The Directive

The purpose of the Directive is presented in the first paragraph of article 1 of the Directive. Its purpose is to facilitate the use of electronic signatures and to contribute to their legal recognition. The Directive establishes a legal framework for electronic signatures and certain certification services in order to ensure the proper functioning of the internal market.

The second paragraph enumerates the fields that the Directive does not cover. It does not cover aspects related to the conclusion and validity of contracts or other legal obligations where there are requirements as regards form prescribed by national or Community law nor does it affect rules and limits, contained in national or Community law, governing the use of documents. This means, for example, that the Directive does not give a solution for statutory requirements of form, which explicitly or implicitly provide that a contract is invalid or unenforceable if parties have not used a hand-written signature.[13] Member States may of course go beyond the scope of the Directive and amend their law in such a way that certain electronic signatures can meet a requirement of a hand-written signature.

4.2 ECA

According to the explanatory notes to the ECA its main purpose is to help build confidence in electronic commerce and the technology underlying it by providing for:

(a) an approvals scheme for businesses and other organisations providing cryptography services, such as electronic signature services and confidentiality services;
(b) the legal recognition of electronic signatures and the process under which they are verified, generated or communicated; and
(c) the removal of obstacles in other legislation to the use of electronic communication and storage in place of paper.

So the ECA provides a legal framework for electronic signatures and certification services for digital signatures.

The ECA does not contain a general provision with regard to statutory requirements of form impeding the electronic performance of juridical acts or the electronic conclusion of contracts in particular. However, section 8 subsection (1) provides that subject to subsection (3), the appropriate Minister may by order made by statutory instrument modify the provisions of:

(a) any enactment or subordinate legislation, or
(b) any scheme, licence, authorisation or approval issued, granted or given by or under any enactment or subordinate legislation,

---

13 For an overview of requirements of form under English law I refer to C. Reed, *Digital information law. Electronic Documents and Requirements of Form* (London: Centre for Commercial Law Studies 1996).

in such manner as he may think fit for the purpose of authorising or facilitating the use of electronic communications or electronic storage (instead of other forms of communication or storage) for any purpose mentioned in subsection (2).

One of the purposes mentioned in subsection (2) is the doing of anything which under any such provisions is required to be or may be authorised by a person's signature or seal, or is required to be delivered as a deed or witnessed.

Subsection (3) provides that the appropriate Minister shall not make an order under section 8 authorising the use of electronic communications for any purpose, unless he considers that the authorisation is such that the extent (if any) to which records of things done for that purpose will be available will be no less satisfactory in cases where use is made of electronic communications or electronic storage than in other cases. When authorising the use of an electronic signature as an alternative for a statutory required hand-written signature the appropriate Minister must therefore ascertain that the authorised electronic signature fulfils the same functions of the hand-written signature as those that the legislator had in mind when it laid down the requirement of a hand-written signature.

Thus section 8 of the ECA empowers Ministers to modify existing legislation that requires a hand-written signature for a certain juridical act.[14] The explanatory notes to the ECA give as an example the modification of the Companies Act 1985 to enable companies to use electronic means to deliver company communications, to receive shareholder proxy and voting instructions and to incorporate.

4.3 DESA

The DESA implements the European Directive on Electronic Signatures. By amending the Dutch Civil Code (DCC), the Dutch Telecommunications Act (TA) and the Dutch Economic Offences Act (EOA) it creates a legal framework for electronic signatures which is in conformity with the European Directive.

The DESA does not contain a provision regarding statutory requirements of form requiring a hand-written signature for the validity or the enforceability of contracts.[15]

---

14 See M. Hogg, 'Secrecy and Signatures- Turning the Legal Spotlight on Encryption and Electronic Signatures', in: L. Edwards & C. Waelde, *Law and the Internet. A Framework for Electronic Commerce* (Oxford: Hart Publications 2000), p. 46-47.

15 This is covered by the Electronic Commerce Bill which was recently presented to parliament. See *Kamerstukken II* 2001/02, 28 197, nr. 1. The Electronic Commerce Bill contains the proposal of the Dutch government to implement the European Directive 2000/31/EC of the European Parliament and of the Council of 8 June 2000 on electronic commerce, OJ 2000 L 178/1. The proposed article 6:227a Dutch Civil Code provides that in case of a statutory requirement of form requiring a writing for the validity of a contract such a contract can be entered into electronically if certain conditions are met. One of these conditions is that the identity of the parties to the contract can be determined with sufficient certainty.

5 MARKET ACCESS

5.1 The Directive

Article 3 of the Directive deals with the access of the market of certification services by certification service providers (CSPs). Member States are prohibited from introducing a licence scheme for certification services. They may, however, introduce or maintain voluntary accreditation schemes aiming at enhanced levels of certification service provision.

The third paragraph of article 3 of the Directive imposes on the Member States the obligation to establish an appropriate system that allows for supervision of CSPs that are established in their territory and issue qualified certificates to the public. A qualified certificate is a certificate that meets the requirements of Annex I of the Directive and is issued by a CSP that fulfils the requirements laid down in Annex II of the Directive.

Certain electronic signatures that are based on a qualified certificate and that are created by a secure signature-creation device will have a special legal status. A secure signature-creation device is a device that fulfils the requirements laid down in Annex III of the Directive. An example of such a secure device is a chip card containing the secret private key of the signer and the algorithms that are used to encrypt the hash value of a message and thus create a digital signature. According to paragraph 4 of article 3 of the Directive each Member State shall ensure that the conformity of secure signature creation devices with the requirements laid down in Annex III of the Directive shall be determined by appropriate public or private bodies designated by the Member State (home State control). A determination of conformity with the requirements by such a body shall be recognised in the other Member States. The home State control and the mutual recognition mean that the access to the market of secure signature-creation devices in the European Union is co-ordinated.

Finally paragraph 7 of article 3 of the Directive provides that Member States may make the use of electronic signatures in the public sector subject to additional requirements. Such requirements must, however, be objective, transparent, proportionate and non-discriminatory and shall relate only to the specific characteristics of the application concerned. They may not constitute an obstacle to cross-border services for citizens.

5.2 ECA

Part I of the ECA deals with cryptography service providers who provide cryptography support services. As explained in paragraph 3.1, digital signatures are based on cryptography.

According to section 6 of the ECA, 'cryptography support service' means any service which is provided to the senders or recipients of electronic communications, or to those storing electronic data, and is designed to facilitate the use of cryptographic techniques for the purpose of, among others, securing that the authenticity or integrity of such communications or data is capable of being ascertained.

This means that Part I of the ECA is also applicable to CSPs issuing certificates for the verification of digital signatures.

Article 3 of the Directive prohibits a licence scheme for CSPs. The ECA introduces a voluntary approval scheme. Section 2 subsection (1) imposes on the Secretary of State the duty to secure that there are arrangements in force for granting approvals to persons who are providing cryptography support services in the United Kingdom or are proposing to do so and seek approval in respect of any such services that they are providing, or are proposing to provide, whether in the United Kingdom or elsewhere.

Pursuant to section 2 subsection (2) paragraph (b) the arrangements must ensure that an approval is granted to a person in respect of any services only if the condition for the grant of an approval to that person is fulfilled in accordance with subsection (3).

According to section 2 subsection (3) paragraph (a) the condition that must be fulfilled before an approval is granted to any person is that the Secretary of State is satisfied that that person, among others, will comply in providing the services in respect of which he is approved, with such technical and other requirements as may be prescribed.

These provisions constitute a voluntary accreditation scheme as mentioned in article 3.2 of the Directive.

Finally section 2 subsection (4) provides that regulations made by virtue of paragraph (a) of subsection (3) may frame a requirement for the purposes of that subsection by reference to the opinion of a person specified in the regulations, or of a person chosen in a manner determined in accordance with the regulations. Pursuant to this provision the Secretary of State can, for example, call in the UK accreditation body to examine whether the person applying for an approval fulfils the technical and other requirements prescribed by the Secretary of State and to give an opinion with respect to the fulfilment to the Secretary of State.

Cryptography service providers that are approved under the scheme described above will be registered in a register of approved providers established and maintained by the Secretary of State pursuant to section 1 subsection (1) of the ECA. Section 1 subsection (4) paragraph (a) provides that the Secretary of State shall ensure that such arrangements are in force as he considers appropriate for allowing members of the public to inspect the contents of the register. Thus anybody receiving an electronic certificate issued by a CSP will be able to consult the register and determine whether the certificate was issued by a CSP approved by the Secretary of State. If the CSP has been approved, such an approval gives the recipient of the certificate some comfort regarding the reliability of the CSP.

5.3 *DESA*

The DESA includes an amendment of the Telecommunications Act (TA). Article 2.1 of the TA deals with CSPs issuing qualified certificates[16] to the public in the Netherlands. If such a CSP has an establishment in the Netherlands it is under the obligation to register with the OPTA. The OPTA is the authority that supervises compliance with the TA by telecommunication service providers. The CSP that applies for a registration must hand over documents that prove that it and its qualified certificates meet the requirements of article 18.15 of the TA. These requirements will be the same requirements as those laid down in Annex I (qualified certificates) and Annex II (CSPs issuing qualified certificates) of the Directive.

Pursuant to article 2.2 of the TA the OPTA can cancel a registration if it determines that a CSP that issues qualified certificates does not or not completely fulfil the requirements for the issuance of such certificates and the CSP has not within a reasonable period of time proven its fulfilment of those requirements.

Article 18.16 of the TA provides for an acknowledgement of private accreditation schemes. It gives the Minister of Transport and Communications the authority to designate one or more organisations that screen CSPs on compliance with the statutory requirements imposed on CSPs issuing qualified certificates.

In the Netherlands a private accreditation scheme has been developed by the Dutch association Electronic Commerce Platform Netherlands (ECP.NL) in co-operation with the Dutch Council for Accreditation. A CSP may apply for accreditation with ECP.NL. The actual screening of the CSP will be performed by certification bodies under the supervision of the Dutch Council of Accreditation, which maintains the criteria for accreditation of CSPs. These criteria are based on the ETSI TS 101 456 policy requirements for certification authorities issuing qualified certificates. When the CSP meets the criteria it will be included in a public register of accredited CSPs. This public register will be accessible for the public through the Internet.[17] This scheme will probably be recognised by the Minister of Transport and Communications under article 18.16 of the TA.

A CSP that has obtained an accreditation from an organisation that has been designated by the Minister of Transport and Communications under article 18.16 of the TA is presumed to fulfil the requirements of article 18.15 of the TA. Furthermore, its qualified certificates are also presumed to fulfil the requirements of article 18.15 of the TA. Based on these two presumptions a CSP that has been accredited does not have to hand over documents proving that it and its certificates meet the requirements of article 18.15 of the TA. According to article 2.1 of the TA it only has to hand over a valid certificate of the designated accreditation organisation acknowledging that it has been accredited.

---

16 See paragraph 3.2 for an explanation of this concept.

17 I refer to the brochure *TTP.NL. Certification in the area of electronic signatures* (Leidschendam: ECP.NL 2001).

Finally, article 18.17 of the TA regulates the access to the market of secure signature-creation devices.[18] Such a device must meet the requirements laid down in an Order in Council. These requirements will be the same as those of Annex III of the Directive. The Minister of Transport and Communications can assign an organisation with the task of assessing whether signature- creation devices fulfil the requirements set by the Order in Council. This may be a foreign organisation. Until now, none of the eligible Dutch organisations have shown any interest in such an assignment.

The amendment of the Dutch Economic Offences Act (EOA) tails the provisions of the TA regarding CSPs issuing qualified certificates and secure-signature-creation devices. Violation of the obligation to register with the OPTA or of article 18.15 and article 18.17 of the TA are qualified as penal offences under article 1 subparagraphs 2 and 4 of the EOA.

6 INTERNAL MARKET PRINCIPLES

6.1 The Directive

Article 4 contains two provisions regarding co-ordination. Article 4.1 lays down the principle of home State control. It provides that each Member State shall apply the national provisions which it adopts pursuant to the Directive to certification service providers established on its territory and to the services which they provide. Furthermore, this article lays down the principle of mutual recognition. Member States may not restrict the provision of certification services originating in another Member State in the fields covered by the Directive. The fields covered by the Directive are described in article 1 of the Directive.[19]

Article 4.2 is based on the principle of free flow of goods, which is one of the main principles of the Treaty establishing the European Community. It provides that Member States shall ensure that electronic-signature products which comply with the Directive are permitted to circulate freely in the internal market. An example of an electronic-signature product is a chip card containing the private key and the algorithms used to generate a digital signature.[20]

6.2 ECA

The ECA does not contain any provisions regarding the principles of home State control and mutual recognition of certification services originating in another Member State. Nor does it include provisions with respect to the principle of free circulation

18 This concept is explained in paragraph 3.2.
19 See paragraph 4.1.
20 See paragraph 3.

of electronic-signature products complying with the Directive. On the other hand, there are no provisions in the ECA contravening these principles.

6.3 *DESA*

The home State control principle is enacted in article 2.1 of the Dutch Telecommunication Act. This article restricts the obligation to register with the OPTA to CSPs having an establishment in the Netherlands. Like the ECA the DESA does not include any provisions regarding the principles of mutual recognition or the free circulation of electronic-signature products nor any provisions contravening these principles.

7 Legal effects of electronic signatures

7.1 *The Directive*

Article 5 is probably the most important article in the Directive. For a long time it was uncertain in most Member States of the European Union what legal effects courts would attribute to an electronic signature. Would courts accept electronic signatures as evidence in legal proceedings? What evidential value would they attribute to electronic signatures? Would courts apply the rebuttable presumption that an electronic document to which the electronic signature of a certain person was attached, was signed by that person until proven otherwise? Would courts derive from the generation of an electronic signature that the person generating that signature expressed his will to be bound to the electronically signed declaration?

Article 5 prevents to some extent that the courts in the different Member States would all answer these questions in a different way. It distinguishes between two categories of electronic signatures: (i) advanced electronic signatures which are based on a qualified certificate[21] and which are created by a secure[22] signature-creation device and (ii) other electronic signatures.

The first category of electronic signatures

According to article 2 of the Directive an advanced electronic signature is a signature that meets the following requirements:

(a) it is uniquely linked to the signatory;
(b) it is capable of identifying the signatory;
(c) it is created using means that the signatory can maintain under his sole control; and
(d) it is linked to the data to which it relates in such a manner that any subsequent change of the data is detectable.

---

21 See paragraph 3.2.
22 See paragraph 3.2.

It is clear that a digital signature is an advanced electronic signature in the meaning of the Directive. A digital signature is uniquely linked to the signatory by the secret private key with which it is generated. The digital signature enables the recipient to verify the identity of the originator. It is created with a secret private key that the signatory can maintain under his sole control. And it is linked to the data because it is based on the hash value that is calculated over the data. Finally, a change of the data can be detected by means of the digital signature because in that case the hash value resulting from the decryption of the digital signature differs from the hash value calculated by the recipient.[23]

Pursuant to article 5.1 of the Directive Member States shall ensure that electronic signatures falling within the first category:
(a) satisfy the legal requirements of a signature in relation to data in electronic form in the same manner as a hand-written signature satisfies those requirements in relation to paper-based data; and
(b) are admissible as evidence in legal proceedings.

Second category of electronic signatures
According to article 5.2 of the Directive Member States shall ensure that an electronic signature is not denied legal effectiveness and admissibility as evidence in legal proceedings solely on the grounds that it is:
(a) in electronic form, or
(b) not based upon a qualified certificate, or
(c) not based upon a qualified certificate issued by an accredited certification-service-provider, or
(d) not created by a secure signature-creation device.

7.2 ECA

Article 5.2 of the Directive is partly implemented in the laws of the UK by section 7 of the ECA. This section provides that in any legal proceedings:

(a) an electronic signature incorporated into or logically associated with a particular electronic communication or particular electronic data, and
(b) the certification by any person of such a signature, shall each be admissible in evidence in relation to any question as to the authenticity of the communication or data or as to the integrity of the communication or data.

Section 15 subsection (2) of the ECA provides that:
(a) references to the authenticity of any communication or data are references to any one or more of the following:
    (i) whether the communication or data comes from a particular person or other source;

23 I refer to paragraph 3.1 for a description of the digital signature.

(ii) whether it is accurately timed and dated;
(iii) whether it is intended to have legal effect;

and

(b) references to the integrity of any communication or data are references to whether there has been any tampering with or other modification of the communication or data.

So the ECA guarantees the admissibility of electronic signatures and electronic certificates issued by CSPs for the verification of digital signatures as evidence in legal proceedings. It does not, however, go into the legal effects of electronic signatures. The validity of electronic signatures has been addressed in terms of their evidential admissibility.[24] A party requesting a court to attribute certain legal effects to an electronic signature, e.g. the authenticity of the electronic communication to which the electronic signature was attached, will have to convince the court that the technology that has been used to create the electronic signature is sufficiently reliable taking into account all circumstances. Parties may of course insert a clause into their interchange agreement[25] with respect to the legal effects that have to be attributed to an electronic signature. In a business-to-consumer relationship such a clause may, however, be set aside by the court if it is an unfair contract term.

7.3 DESA

The Dutch legislator has chosen a generic approach with regard to the legal recognition of electronic signatures. The new article 3:15a paragraph 1 of the Dutch Civil Code (DCC) will provide that an electronic signature will have the same legal effect as a hand-written signature if the method of authentication that has been used is sufficiently reliable taking into account the purpose for which the electronic data has been used and all other relevant circumstances.

According to article 3:15a paragraph 2 of the DCC a method for authentication is presumed to be sufficiently reliable if it is an advanced electronic signature[26] based on a qualified certificate[27] and created with a secure signature-creation device.[28]

Finally article 3:15a paragraph 3 of the DCC provides that a method for authentication may not be regarded as insufficiently reliable on the sole ground that:

(a) It is not based on a qualified certificate;
(b) It is not based on a certificate issued by a CSP that fulfils the requirements of article 18.16 of the TA;
(c) It has not been created with a secure signature-creation device.

---

24 M. Hogg 2000, p. 45 (see note 15).

25 An interchange agreement is an agreement regarding the electronic interchange of data between two or more parties. See A.H. Boss and J. Ritter, *Electronic Data Interchange Agreements. A Guide and Sourcebook* (Paris: International Chamber of Commerce 1993).

26 See paragraph 7.1.

27 See paragraph 5.3.

28 See paragraph 5.3.

Article 3:15a paragraph 6 of the DCC provides that parties may deviate from paragraph 2 and 3 by contract. The court can, however, set aside a clause in an agreement regarding the legal effects of an electronic signature if it is a clause in the general conditions of one party and the clause is unreasonably onerous towards the other party (article 6: 233 DCC[29]) or if the clause is unacceptable according to the criteria of reasonableness and fairness (article 6:248 BW), all circumstances taken into account.

8 Liability of CSP

8.1 *The Directive*

A CSP issues electronic certificates. A certificate contains the public key of the sender of an electronic message. The recipient can verify the digital signature of the sender that has been attached to an electronic message by decrypting the digital signature with the public key of the sender.[30]

The CSP can make several mistakes in the process of issuing a certificate or managing certificates. The CSP can, for example, issue a certificate without verifying the identity of the person applying for the certificate. Or the information in the certificate itself can be incorrect. The CSP can also fail to include a revoked certificate in the Certificates Revocation List. Such mistakes can cause loss to the holder of the certificate or to a third party that relies on the certificate. In the first case there will be a contractual relationship between the holder of the certificate and the CSP. This contract is usually governed by the general conditions of the CSP contained in the Certificate Policy of the CSP. A third party relying on the certificate when verifying the digital signature of the sender of an electronic message does not necessarily have a contractual relationship with the issuer of the certificate. In that case the question whether the CSP is liable towards that third party for loss sustained by that party as a result of a mistake of the CSP must be answered on the basis of the law of tort.

In some cases a certificate is guaranteed by another CSP than the CSP that has issued the certificate. Such a guarantee may occur if the issuing CSP is insufficiently known in the country of the guaranteeing CSP to create trust with possible third parties in that country that have to rely on the certificate for the verification of a digital signature. In that case the question with regard to the liability of the issuing CSP towards relying parties for loss resulting from a mistake of the issuing CSP is extended to a question of liability of the guaranteeing CSP.

The Directive contains a provision regarding the liability of the CSP towards third parties relying on a certificate issued or guaranteed by that CSP. Article 6 paragraph 1 of the Directive provides that as a minimum, Member States shall ensure that by issuing a certificate as a qualified certificate to the public or by guaranteeing such a cer-

29 There are some exceptions to this rule e.g. if the other party is a large enterprise.

30 I refer to figure 2 of paragraph 3.

tificate to the public a CSP is liable for damage caused to any entity or legal or natural person who reasonably relies on that certificate:

(a) as regards the accuracy at the time of issuance of all information contained in the qualified certificate and as regards the fact that the certificate contains all the details prescribed for a qualified certificate;
(b) for assurance that at the time of the issuance of the certificate, the signatory identified in the qualified certificate held the signature-creation data corresponding to the signature-verification data given or identified in the certificate;
(c) for assurance that the signature-creation data and the signature-verification data can be used in a complementary manner in cases where the CSP generates them both;

unless the CSP proves that it has not acted negligently.

It is important to notice that the provision in article 6 is restricted to parties relying on the certificate for the verification of a digital signature. This provision does not cover the liability towards the holder of the certificate. Furthermore the provision is restricted to CSPs issuing or guaranteeing a qualified certificate.[31] Finally it is restricted to qualified certificates issued to the public. In case of a closed system of issuance of certificates which is not open to the public the provision does not apply. If a situation does not fall within the scope of this provision the liability of the CSP for loss occurred by a relying party will have to established on the basis of the law of tort.

Article 6 paragraph 1 provides that the CSP is not liable if it can prove that it has not acted negligently. Thus, a CSP has not violated a duty of care towards relying parties if it has verified the identity of the holder of the certificate by means of his passport, the passport has been forged or falsified and the CSP could not reasonably have detected such a forgery or falsification by checking the passport and any available registries of stolen or missing passports.

Sub-paragraph (c) of article 6 paragraph 1 refers to the situation in which the CSP generates the key pair, i.e. the secret private key and the corresponding public key. In most cases the holder of the certificate will have generated the key pair himself. For the issuance of the certificate the holder will only have presented the public key to the CSP. However, in some systems the CSP generates the key pair. In that case the CSP is liable towards relying third parties if the private key and the public key are not complementary.

Article 6 paragraph 2 contains a provision regarding the liability of the issuing CSP for failure to include a revoked qualified certificate in the Certificates Revocation List maintained by that CSP or a third party maintaining such a registration on behalf of the CSP. A certificate can, for example, be revoked by the holder if he detects that one or more instruments, like the secret private key, which are being used for generating the digital signature have been compromised because an unauthorised third party has obtained them. Article 6 paragraph 2 provides that, as a minimum, Member

---

31 See paragraph 3.2.

States shall ensure that a CSP that has issued a certificate as a qualified certificate to the public is liable for damage caused to any entity or legal or natural person who reasonably relies on the certificate for failure to register revocation of the certificate unless the CSP proves that it has not acted negligently. With respect to this provision the same restrictions apply as with regard to article 6 paragraph 1.

Articles 6 paragraphs 3 and 4 provide the CSP that issues qualified certificates with a possibility to restrict its liability towards relying third parties by indicating in the certificate that its use is limited to certain transactions or to transactions not exceeding a certain value. In that case the CSP will not be liable for transactions outside the indicated limitation, provided that such a limitation was recognisable to third parties.

Finally, article 6 paragraph 5 provides that the provisions of article 6 shall be without prejudice to the European Directive on unfair terms in consumer contracts.[32]

8.2 ECA

The ECA has not implemented article 6 of the Directive. The British government has decided that it need not amend existing law to fulfil its obligation under article 6 of the Directive.[33]

8.3 DESA

The Dutch legislator has fulfilled its obligations under article 6 of the Directive by inserting art. 6:196b into the Dutch Civil Code. As these provisions do not fundamentally differ from those of article 6 of the Directive I will not go into them.

9 Cross-border recognition of qualified certificates

9.1 The Directive

Qualified certificates issued within the European Union must be recognised by the Member States. This follows from the principle of free flow of services laid down in the Treaty establishing the European Community. Furthermore article 4 paragraph 1 provides that Member States may not restrict the provision of certification services originating in another Member State in the fields covered by the Directive. The fields covered by the Directive are described in article 1 of the Directive.

But what if the qualified certificate was issued by a CSP in a third country? Article 7

32 Directive 93/13/EEC of 5 April 1993 on unfair terms in consumer contracts, OJ 1993 L 95/29.
33 M. Hogg 2000, p. 48-49 (see note 15).

paragraph 1 lays down the situations in which a Member State must recognise such a certificate. It provides that

Member States shall ensure that certificates which are issued as qualified certificates to the public by a CSP established in a third country are recognised as legally equivalent to certificates issued by a CSP established within the Community if:

(1) the CSP fulfils the requirements laid down in the Directive and has been accredited under a voluntary accreditation scheme[34] established in a Member State; or
(2) a CSP established within the Community which fulfils the requirements laid down in the Directive guarantees the certificate;[35] or
(3) the certificate or the CSP is recognised under a bilateral or multilateral agreement between the Community and third countries or international organisations.

9.2 *ECA*

The ECA does not contain a provision regarding the recognition of certificates issued in a third country.

9.3 *DESA*

The proposed article 3:15b of the Dutch Civil Code implements article 7 of the Directive. Its provisions are similar to those in the Directive, so I will not go into them.

10 DATA PROTECTION

10.1 *The Directive*

CSPs issuing certificates to natural persons will process personal data with regard to such persons. They may, for example, collect and/or register the name, the address, the passport number, the public key and, in some cases, the private key from the applicants. Data may be collected and registered because a national regulation imposes an obligation to collect and register on the CSP. Thus, a legislator may have imposed an obligation on national CSPs to register private keys to enable authorities investigating crime or preserving national security to access electronic messages or other data that have been encrypted with the public key of the recipient: the so-called legal access. Another reason for processing personal data can be that the CSP needs these data to execute the contract that it has concluded with the holder of the certificate. The name and address may be necessary to send the holder of the certificate an invoice for the services rendered. The CSP can also collect and register data for evi-

34 See paragraph 5.1.
35 See paragraph 8.1.

dential purposes. One may think of the passport number it needs to have when a relying third party holds it liable for loss suffered. It must then be able to prove that it has not acted negligently. So the CSP may have many valid reasons to process personal data; reasons that have been recognised by the European Privacy Directive.[36]

Article 8 paragraph 1 of the Directive on electronic signatures provides that Member States shall ensure that CSPs and national bodies responsible for accreditation or supervision comply with the requirements laid down in the European Privacy Directive.

In addition to this Privacy Directive article 8 paragraph 2 provides that Member States shall ensure that a CSP which issues certificates to the public may collect personal data only directly from the data subject, or after the explicit consent of the data subject, and only insofar as it is necessary for the purposes of issuing and maintaining the certificate. The data may not be collected or processed for any other purposes without the explicit consent of the data subject. This provision does not, for example, prohibit the CSP from obtaining access to a registry of stolen or missing passports to check the validity of a passport presented to it by an applicant as long as the CSP does not collect data from this registry. The purposes for which the CSP can collect data are too restricted, in my view. For instance, Article 8 paragraph 2 seems to exclude for example the collection of personal data for evidential purposes whereas article 7, paragraph f of the European Privacy Directive allows such a processing of personal data.

Users of the Internet leave behind a digital trail. This allows others to collect a large number of personal data with regard to an Internet user. One way to prevent this is by using anonymous certificates. Article 8 paragraph 3 of the Directive on electronic signatures refers to another way of averting digital trails: using certificates with a pseudonym. It provides that without prejudice to the legal effect given to pseudonyms under national law, Member States shall not prevent CSPs from indicating in the certificate a pseudonym instead of the signatory's name. One should realise, however, that in many cases the party relying on the certificate has a reasonable interest in obtaining personal data from the other party or must have the name and address of the other party to be able to execute the contract concluded with the other party.

For instance, an Internet seller selling software that can be downloaded by the buyer, for example, must have some personal data of the buyer when it enters into a licence agreement with that buyer. Certificates with a pseudonym could be useful, for example, if the certificate is used to obtain access to a data bank and payment is made directly by means of electronic money.

36 Directive 95/46/EC of the European Parliament and of the Council of 24 October 1995 on the protection of individuals with regard to the processing of personal data and on the free movement of such data, OJ 1995 L 281/31.

10.2 ECA

The ECA only implements article 8 paragraph 1 of the Directive. Section 4 subsection (1) provides that no information which:

(a) has been obtained under or by virtue of the provisions of part I of the ECA, and
(b) relates to the private affairs of any individual or to any particular business,

shall, during the lifetime of that individual or so long as that business continues to be carried on, be disclosed without the consent of that individual or the person for the time being carrying on that business.

Pursuant to subsection (2) subsection (1) does not apply to any disclosure of information which is made:

(a) for the purpose of facilitating the carrying out of any functions under part I of the ECA, or any prescribed functions, of the Secretary of State or a person appointed under section 3 of the ECA;
(b) for the purpose of facilitating the carrying out of any functions of a local weights and measures authority in Great Britain;
(c) for the purpose of facilitating the carrying out of prescribed public functions of any person;
(d) in connection with the investigation of any criminal offence or for the purposes of any criminal proceedings;
(e) for the purposes of any civil proceedings which
    (i) relate to the provision of cryptography support services; and
    (ii) are proceedings to which a person approved in accordance with arrangements under section 2 is a party; or
(f) in pursuance of a Community obligation.

According to subsection (6) any person who discloses any information in contravention of this section shall be guilty of an offence and liable:

(a) on summary conviction, to a fine not exceeding the statutory maximum;
(b) on conviction on indictment, to imprisonment for a term not exceeding two years or a fine, or to both.

Article 8 paragraph 2 of the Directive is not implemented by the ECA.

10.3 DESA

The Dutch government proposes to implement article 8 paragraph 2 of the Directive by inserting article 11.5a into the Dutch Telecommunications Act. The provisions of this article are identical to those of article 8.2 of the Directive.

Implementation of the other provisions of article 8 of the Directive is considered to be unnecessary because they are already covered by existing law.

11 Closing remarks

One of the important objectives of the Directive is the harmonisation of the laws of the Member States regarding the legal recognition of electronic signatures, the liability of CSPs and the protection of personal data disclosed by an applicant for a certificate to a CSP. Bearing this in mind it is remarkable that the UK government and the Dutch government have each taken a different approach in implementing this Directive. Whereas the Dutch government has chosen for a nearly complete implementation, the UK government has decided not to insert provisions into the ECA with respect to the legal effects of electronic signatures, the liability of CSPs issuing qualified certificates and the protection of personal data provided by an applicant to a CSP. However, this does not necessarily mean that the laws of the UK and the Netherlands with regard to these topics will strongly deviate from each other. Construction and application of national rules of law in conformity with European Directives can prevent the objective of harmonisation from not being achieved.[37]

37 See M.H. Wissink, *Richtlijnconforme interpretatie van burgerlijk recht* (Deventer: Kluwer 2001), p. 50.

Civil liability of Internet providers following the Directive on Electronic Commerce

*Cyril van der Net**

1 INTRODUCTION

Section 4 of Directive 2000/31/EC of the European Parliament and of the Council of 8 June 2000 on certain legal aspects of information society services, in particular electronic commerce, in the Internal Market ('Directive on electronic commerce') includes a liability regulation for information society service providers who act as intermediaries (Internet providers).[1] Although the liability regulation has a horizontal tenor, meaning that the Directive has implications for public law as well as private law, this contribution deals with the private law questions sparked by the regulation.[2] The fact that the Directive raises certain questions does not alter the fact that the attempt should be appreciated. The Internet mocks country borders. Therefore, regulation of the medium should occur at an international, preferably global and in any case community level.[3]

2 NON-LIABILITY

Unlawful acts can be committed through the supply of Internet provider services. This raises the question whether Internet providers can be called to account for this. The Directive does not answer this question. What it does indicate is under which conditions and circumstances an intermediary cannot be held liable. The Directive creates three 'free havens', differentiating according to the service or activity performed by the Internet provider. When an Internet provider cannot benefit from such an exemption from liability, we must answer the question as to whether he can be held liable, and if so to what extent, by using the general national doctrines of the unlawful act. An answer to liability questions is closely intertwined with the specific circumstances of the case.

---

* This contribution was written in Van der Net's personal capacity.

1 OJ, 17 July 2000m L 178.

2 On criminal implications see: C.B. van der Net, *Grenzen stellen op het Internet, Aansprakelijkheid van Internet-providers en rechtsmacht* (Setting boundaries on the Internet, Liability of Internet providers and Jurisdiction), (dissertation Leiden University, Gouda: Quint, 2000).

3 *Kamerstukken II* (Parliamentary Papers II), 1997-1998, 25 880, vol. 1-2, p. 180.

H. Snijders, S. Weatherill (eds.), *E-commerce Law*, 49-57

2.1 *Mere conduit*

In a case of 'mere conduit' (article 12 of the Directive), the Internet provider merely acts as a serving hatch. This is the case when he merely transmits information or provides access to the Internet. When the Internet provider does not initiate the transmission, does not select the recipient of the service and does not modify or select the information contained in the transmission, he cannot be held liable. The rationale of liability exemption for 'mere conduit' is that the Internet provider's action in that case is of a merely technical, automatic and passive nature. This implies that he does not have knowledge of and control over the transmitted information. When the Internet provider deliberately engages in a cooperation with an information provider who is responsible for the contents of the transmitted information in order to commit an unlawful act, the Internet provider can no longer benefit from the exemption from liability (see consideration 44).

2.2 *Caching*

'Caching' (article 13 of the Directive) is an activity which consists of the automatic, intermediate and temporary storage of information performed for the sole purpose of making more efficient the information's onward transmission to other recipients of the service upon their request. There is no liability if five cumulative conditions are met. First, the Internet provider must not modify the temporarily stored information. Second, the Internet provider should comply with conditions on access to the information. Thirdly, he should comply with widely recognised and used rules regarding the updating of the information. In addition, he should not infringe the widely recognised and used rules of technology to obtain data on the use of information.[4] Finally, he should remove the information as soon as he knows that it has been removed from the initial source on the communication network or access to it has been disabled, or that a court or an administrative authority has ordered the removal of the information or that its access be disabled. As is the case with 'mere conduit', the Internet provider's exemption from liability for 'caching' is based on the fact that the Internet provider's actions in those cases are of a merely technical, automatic and passive nature.

2.3 *Hosting*

'Hosting' is a service consisting of the storage of information provided by a recipient of the service. Liability for hosting (article 14 of the Directive) does not exist as long as the Internet provider does not have actual knowledge of facts or circumstances

---

4 This concerns so-called counters. An information provider's web page often contains adverts, which can be clicked on. The information provider often receives a fee for these adverts, which can be based, among other things, on the number of times the advert is clicked through. Clicking through from and to a copy should be taken into consideration. The service provider must not modify the technology used for this.

showing the unlawful nature of information (article 14 paragraph 1 of the Directive). The Internet provider acting as 'host' is not liable either, when he, upon having or obtaining such knowledge, acts expeditiously to remove or to disable access to the information. The exemption does not apply when the recipient of the Internet provider's service is acting under the authority or the control of the Internet provider (article 14 paragraph 2 of the Directive).

3 PROHIBITORY INJUNCTION

The three kinds of exemptions from liability mentioned above shall not affect the possibility for a legal authority to require the Internet provider to terminate or prevent an infringement (article 12 paragraph 3, article 13 paragraph 2, article 14 paragraph 3 of the Directive, respectively). For this a so-called prohibitory injunction can be carried out.

4 NO GENERAL MONITORING OBLIGATION

In the case of mere conduit, caching and hosting, Internet providers are not subject to a general obligation to monitor the information transmitted through their provided services or to actively search for facts or circumstances indicating unlawful activity (article 15 paragraph 1). From further considerations about this we can deduce that certain duties of care can exist in special cases where the Internet provider who stores information has reasonable doubt regarding the lawfulness of the information stored by him in connection with the justified interests of third parties (see, for example, considerations 47 and 48). Member States may establish obligations for Internet providers we know about or are informed of alleged unlawful activities, to report this to the competent authorities (article 15 paragraph 2). Member States may also establish obligations to provide data whereby the information provider responsible for the information's content can be identified. According to the letter of the Directive, this latest obligation is limited to hosting (article 15 paragraph 2). I will return to this in paragraph 8.

5 NO WATERTIGHT PARTITIONS

The liability regulation described above ties in with certain activities, i.e. mere conduit, caching and hosting respectively. The boundary between mere conduit and caching is continuous. This is caused by the fact that the term 'mere conduit' also covers the automatic, intermediary and temporary storage of information, in so far as this takes place for the sole purpose of making the information easier to transmit and provided that the information is not stored for any period longer than is reasonably necessary for the transmission (article 12 paragraph 2 of the Directive). The difference with 'caching' probably lies in the fact that the information is not stored for the purpose of others who request this information.

The boundary between caching and hosting is also not always an easy one to draw. The Internet provider who simultaneously stores information to make its subsequent transmission more efficient (caching), should comply with the rules regarding the updating of the information that are widely recognised and used by the industry. It is not impossible that the judge in a specific case comes to the conclusion that the Internet provider who does not comply with such technology and customs recognised and used by the industry, stored information in a capacity of host, and therefore the rules regarding hosting apply to him.

6 Dissimilar exemptions

Therefore, we cannot place watertight partitions between the different activities. However, the implications of the difference are considerable. The conditions and circumstances that need to be observed to remain exempt from liability differ from activity to activity. And there is more. The exemptions from liability are dissimilar. The exemptions for mere conduit (article 12 of the Directive) and hosting (article 14 of the Directive) protect the Internet provider from liability for damage resulting from the unlawful nature of the information originating from someone else. The exemption for caching (article 13 of the Directive), however, protects the Internet provider against liability for damage resulting from the temporary storage of information as such. It concerns an exemption from liability in relation to the information provider who is responsible for the content of the information offered. In fact, this concerns the Internet provider's own actions or absence thereof: he is not fulfilling a genuinely intermediary role.[5]

An example might clarify the exemption for caching. The information provider responsible for the content of the information can earmark the information he discloses via the Internet. By making conditions to access the information provided by him, the party responsible for it can prevent, for example, that an agreement on outdated conditions is entered into. By means of the earmark the information provider can make it clear that before it has been verified at the source that the information is correct, the information must not be transmitted from the Internet provider's proxy cache memory. The Internet provider who practises caching should meet such instructions, if he wishes to successfully call on the exemption from liability.

Of course the question arises what happens when unlawful information is cached. In my opinion, it is defendable that the non-liability regulation regarding caching is not applicable here. The question whether there is any liability and if so, to what extent, should be determined by using the general doctrine of the unlawful act, except where exemption for mere conduit or hosting applies.

5 Cf. M.H.M. Schellekens, *Aansprakelijkheid van Internetaanbieders* (Liability of Internet providers), (dissertation Katholieke Universiteit Brabant, Den Haag: SDU 2001).

7 Caching and the act of reproduction protected by copyright law and related rights

There is a transverse connection between the non-liability regulation regarding caching detailed in the Directive on electronic commerce (article 13 of the Directive) and the reproduction right mentioned in the Directive 2001/29/EG of the European Parliament and the Council of 22 May 2001 regarding certain aspects of copyright law and related rights in information society (to which we shall refer as the copyright Directive).[6] Based on article 2 of the copyright Directive, Member States shall provide the exclusive right to authorise or prohibit direct or indirect, temporary or permanent reproduction by any means and in any form. To cache materials protected by copyright law and related rights is an act of reproduction in the sense of article 2 of the copyright Directive.

Based on article 5 paragraph 1 of the copyright Directive, exemptions from the reproduction right are provided for temporary acts of reproduction which are transient or incidental and part of a technological process whose sole purpose is to enable: (a) a transmission in a network between third parties by an intermediary, or (b) a lawful use of a work or other protected material. Furthermore, this act of reproduction must not have any independent economic significance. As is shown in consideration 33, in the usual cases caching will be fall under the limitation specified in article 5 paragraph 1 of the copyright Directive. For this some conditions mentioned in consideration 33 must be met. These conditions are also mentioned in article 13 of the Directive on electronic commerce. The Internet provider must not modify the information and he must not interfere with the lawful use of technology widely recognised and used by the industry in order to obtain data on the use of the information.

If by copyright law and related rights, an act of reproduction is not being committed with regard to caching, the Internet provider cannot be held liable for this. So it seems that both Directives are equally consistent. However, the reproduction right and its related exception for purely technical copies are remarkably not valid for databases and software. Except for the (implicit) consent of the rightholder (see consideration 33 of the copyright Directive), which can perhaps be derived from the earmark attached to the information, it probably cannot be prevented that caching of databases and software results in a relevant act of exploitation by the Internet provider. On the basis of article 13 of the Directive on electronic commerce, Internet providers can nonetheless not be held liable for this. This construction is not a very elegant one.[7]

8 Technology-dependent regulations and the fast changing state of technology

The Internet provider who merely serves as a serving hatch (article 12 of the Directive) is almost categorically excluded from liability. Especially in a fast-changing technological environment, this is not wise. We can already think of cases now for

---

6 OJ, 22 June 2001, L167.

7 P. B. Hugenholtz & K. J. Koelman, 'Copyright Aspects of Caching', EIPR (2000), p. 482-493.

which that would lead to remarkable results, to say the least. One example is that due to fast technological developments in the disclosure of information via a communication network, the interference of a host is no longer strictly necessary: the party responsible for the content of the information, also named the information provider, can be his own host. In order to disclose damaging information, it suffices to enter into an agreement with an Internet provider, who gives him access to the Internet on which his information is transmitted. However, if this Internet provider is alerted to the information's unlawful nature by a third party, whereby the validity of the notification is beyond reasonable doubt, he can act proportionally to prevent further damage. All he needs to do is to deny the information provider concerned access to the network. The alleged factual impossibility for Internet providers who carry out mere conduit activities to act proportionally against the transmission of unlawful information, was one of the most important reasons for the exemption from liability as it was assigned to these Internet providers in the Directive. Under certain circumstances it may be argued that the Internet provider who neglects to act even though he is capable of doing so, is purposely assisting the information provider in committing an unlawful act. In that case the free haven is not applicable.

There are more examples of technology-dependent formulations. Based on article 15 paragraph 2 of the Directive, Internet providers can be obliged to provide information with which the recipients of their service can be identified. According to the letter of the Directive, this possibility is limited to Internet providers who have entered into 'storage agreements' with the recipients of their service (hosting). However, it is obvious that this provision should not be followed to the letter, but in the spirit of the Directive. After all, the example used in the previous paragraph also illustrates that in certain circumstances Internet providers who have entered into transmission agreements with the receivers of their services (mere conduit) are also proportionally capable of this and should therefore be obliged by law to do so. For reasons of legal certainty, technology-independent regulation, as described in the memorandum 'Wetgeving voor de elektronische snelweg (Legislation for the electronic highway)', would have been preferred.[8]

9 Liability and prohibitory injunction

The Internet provider carrying out actions of mere conduit, cannot be held liable (article 12 of the Directive). The rationale of this exemption is that he is usually not aware of the unlawful information he is transmitting or to which he is providing access. Even if he is aware of it, for example because a third party has alerted him to it, he does not have sufficient reasonable means to do something about it. The Radikall case constitutes a perfect example. In this case, the united German access providers (mere conduit) tried to block the left-wing extremist magazine Radikall, which was stored at a Dutch service provider (host). In practice this appeared possible only by blocking the entire domain of the Dutch provider. Because of this, messaging traffic from this domain from and to Germany had become completely impossible. Such dispropor-

---

8 *Kamerstukken II* (Parliamentary Papers II), 1997-1998, 25 880, vol. 1-2, p. 25-26.

tionate measures cannot reasonably be expected from the provider who carries out mere conduit activities, especially considering the horizontal tenor of the constitutionally guaranteed freedom of expression. It must be reasonably possible to act, which only happens if we can act proportionally, with personal and technical measures and at an acceptable cost. Such a situation will not occur very often, but is perfectly conceivable, as indicated in the previous section. The unqualified exemption from liability, meaning Internet providers who only need to comply with a number of rather factual obligations, has therefore been criticised. A prohibitory injunction by a judge can probably offer a solution here (article 12 paragraph 3 of this Directive). The Internet provider carrying out mere conduit activities can be held liable when he ignores such a prohibitory injunction. Here, the liability is based on ignoring a judicial injunction. The non-liability regulations from article 12 paragraph 1 described above presuppose that such an Internet provider cannot have knowledge of, nor control over, the transmitted information. The prohibitory injunction created when this factually incorrect supposition was made, is somewhat alienating: the possibility of a prohibitory injunction basically presupposes knowledge – due to the judicial injunction – as well as control with regard to the damaging information against which proportional measures are to be taken.

10 Compensation claims or declarative judgement

The liability regime for hosting (article 14 of the Directive) seems to suggest that a declaratory judgement can be obtained only if the Internet provider has actual knowledge. However, in a compensation claim it is sufficient to prove that the Internet provider should reasonably know. It is alienating to see that despite the more extensive implications, the conditions here are not as strict. I find it hard not to get the impression that this is a flaw that slipped into the Directive because the Directive is set up in mirror image. The regulations indicate when one cannot be held liable rather than when one can be held liable. In practice, fortunately, this should not pose too many problems. For compensation claims, even when they involve symbolic amounts, judges will use the easier test of whether the intermediary should have reasonably known about the damaging information.

11 Lacunae

The Internet provider storing information provided by another party (hosting ex article 14 of the Directive), is usually capable of acting proportionally and adequately against the information stored by him. From a practical standpoint it is noted that the Internet provider is at risk of having to choose between two evils. The Internet provider who does not make the information inaccessible is in danger of being found liable on account of unlawful action. The Internet provider who does make the information inaccessible risks a claim for default from the receiver of his service. The Internet provider is in effect stuck with weighing the importance of the unlawful information resulting in (potentially) injured parties and the importance of the receivers of his service, usually his contractual counterpart. Here the tension is felt between the importance of the freedom of information on the one hand and the prevention of undesirable forms of content control on the other. The Directive does not provide for a detailed regulation regarding so-called 'notice and take down' procedures to deal with that problem.[9] In my view, at present we should not expect any insurmountable problems in this respect as far as the Netherlands are concerned. The importance of the free exchange of information in society and the increasingly important role of the electronic highway in this area, mean that we can merely request the Internet provider to remove the information or to render it inaccessible if there is no reasonable doubt on its unlawful nature.[10] With regard to notice and take down procedures, the Directive does not contain more than a request to the Member States to encourage the development of such procedures by all parties concerned. Finland has even included a detailed notice and take down procedure into its legislation. The United States also have legal regulations in this field.[11]

Another lacuna that has not yet been mentioned before concerns the lack of an increasingly more important non-liability regulation for providers of hyperlinks and location tools. The United States does have laws on hyperlink and location tool providers. In Europe the liability of the latter Internet providers should be exclusively met on the basis of the general doctrine of the unlawful act.[12]

12 The country of origin principle

On the basis of article 3 of the Directive on electronic commerce, services provided from a European Member State are subject by exclusion to the national legislation of the Member State where the service provider is located (country of origin principle).[13] So the legislation of the country of origin of the Internet provider is applicable to the provided services of the Internet provider. The Internet provider's services can again be used to offer another service for the information company. That service is also subject to the country of origin principle, based on article 3 of the Directive. The question arises whether we cannot avoid the country of origin principle in relation to a(n international) service offered through the Internet provider's services, by addressing the Internet provider. A Dutch judge ordering a Dutch Internet provider to halt transmission of adverts which are unlawful by Dutch law, but are featured on a French company's website, might have as a consequence that the service offered by

---

9 R. J. Julia-Barcelo & K.J. Koelman, 'Intermediary Liability, *Computer & Law Security Report'* (2000), p. 231-239, have argued for the foundation of a special European institution which instead of the Internet providers, should make decisions regarding alleged unlawful information.

10 Cf. Rb. 's Gravenhage 9 June 1999, *Computerrecht* (Computer Law) (1999), p. 200-205.

11 See: Z. de Jongh & L. Siemerink, 'Amerikaanse en Finse elementen voor de Nederlandse implementatie van de Richtlijn inzake Elektronische handel' (American and Finish elements for the implementation of the Directive on Electronic Commerce), *Computerrecht* (Computer Law) (2002), p. 12-20.

12 In the KazaA-case, the Dutch napster without a central database though, the Internet provider was held liable for copyright infringement in first instance. Pres. Rb. Amsterdam, 29 November 2001, AMI (2002) 1, p. 21-25. Recently the Court of Appeals overturned that decision.

13 See the contribution of S. Weatherill in this book.

the French company, even though it is solely subject to French law and so can be completely compliant, can no longer be continued for its Dutch recipients.[14]

13 TO THE EUROPEAN DRAWING BOARD

As far as I am aware, nearly all Member States choose to adopt the liability regulation almost literally. This does not put an end to the discussion though. On the contrary, in addition to the cases mentioned above, in which the text of the Directive or the rationale very clearly at its core already allow for different interpretations, the Directive in article 21 offers a re-examination provision. As shown in article 21 paragraph 2, the evaluation report should examine the need for proposals concerning the liability of providers of Internet providers offering hyperlinks and location tool services. The report should also analyse the possibility of and the need for procedures for notice and take down procedures and the attribution of liability following the taking down of content. Finally, the report should also pay attention to the current need for non-liability regulations for mere conduit and caching to include additional conditions in the light of technological developments. It is recommended that regulations be formulated as technologically independently as possible, so that they can sway along the waves of the ever changing state of technology. At the same time we must be vigilant that those waves of innovation do not use the regulations as their plaything. In that respect it is advisable at the European drawing board to uphold the standard criteria on knowledge and control that have traditionally underpinned liability law.

14 Otherwise: B.J. Drijber, 'De Richtlijn elektronische handel op de snijtafel' (The Directive on electronic commerce on the cutting table), SEW (2001), p. 122-138.

Downloading torts: An English introduction to on-line torts

Roderick Bagshaw

1 Introduction: Torts involving electronic communication

Nobody doubts that torts which can be committed by communication or by delivery of a shoddy service will be capable of being committed by electronic communication. Thus there are already cases dealing with defamation by e-mail and breach of confidence by posting private details on electronic bulletin-boards.[1] Where there are more doubts it is usually because there are doubts about the off-line law: For instance, whether trespass to the person (assault) can be committed by electronic communication will run into the debate about whether it can be committed by words alone.[2] Similarly, claims for violation of privacy interests by electronic intrusion or disclosure of information electronically will have to cope with uncertainty over the extent to which English tort law protects such interests.[3]

Rather than identify every difficult question of English tort law which may arise in an on-line context this contribution concentrates on four issues:

- How far those offering advice or professional services electronically will be subject to tort liability for negligence;
- How the English law of tort will deal with defective electronic products;
- Liability for culpable encouragement of wrongdoing by others and culpable failure to control others; and
- Torts involving damage to e-businesses.

The first three issues involve possible liability to persons who are not beneficiaries of e-contracts but are nonetheless injured by e-commerce or other on-line interactions, whilst the fourth involves injury to e-businesses by persons other than contracting parties.

1 E.g. *Sir Elton John* v. *Countess Joulebine* (QBD, 26.01.2001).

2 See e.g. *Thomas* v. *National Union of Mineworkers (South Wales Area)* [1986] 1 ch. 20.

3 At the time of writing the different views expressed by different members of the Court of Appeal have not been reconciled. Compare, *Douglas* v. *Hello! Ltd* [2001] QB 967, *per* Sedley LJ at [110] ('we have reached a point where it can be said with confidence that the law recognizes and will appropriately protect a right of personal privacy') with *Home Office* v. *Wainwright* [2001] EWCA Civ 2081, *per* Buxton LJ at [114] ('it is still the law of England that there is no tort of invasion of privacy'). In *Campbell* v. *MGN Ltd* [2002] EWCA 1373 counsel for the claimant distinguished between infringement of privacy as a species of breach of confidence and infringement of privacy as a free-standing tort (para. 31). It seems that the former is now well-established in English law (e.g. *A* v. *B* [2002] 3 WLR 542) but the existence of the latter is still unsettled.

H. Snijders, S. Weatherill (eds.), *E-commerce Law*, 59-78

2 Torts in situations 'akin to contract'

It is appropriate to start this section with the observation that professionals and experts may choose to provide services, such as advice, on-line without contracting for payment. They may do this out of altruism, or because they are receiving (or expect to receive) indirect benefits. For instance, the operator of a free-to-consult advice site may receive payments from advertisers, or may hope that some proportion of free-users will be attracted into subsequently making contracts in order to obtain some additional benefit. In such contexts English tort law will have to determine whether the service-provider is subject to an obligation to provide the advice or service to a reasonably competent standard. It is also worth noting that such tort obligations may arise (i) where there is a concluded agreement,[4] but possibly (ii) at a different stage in negotiations from when any agreement was concluded.

The basic rule is that English tort law imposes tort duties on those who profess to have special knowledge or expertise both concurrently with contractual duties to take reasonable care and *also* where the relationship is not contractual but 'akin to contract', or where, using an alternative prominent phrase intended to capture the same idea, there has been 'an assumption of responsibility'. The concept of 'assumption of responsibility' in the law of tort, like that of 'agreement' in the law of contract, is objective.[5] Even an obvious and express indication of unwillingness to assume legal responsibility may not be enough to prevent the conclusion that responsibility has been assumed, since such an express indication may be treated as equivalent to an exclusion clause.[6] It is easier to identify what factors are relevant to determining whether there has been 'an assumption of responsibility' than to provide a mechanical test for such a conclusion. Below, four factors are identified, and some comments made about their importance in the context of on-line advice and service provision.

Individuality. English law is terrified of imposing 'indeterminate liabilities'. Consequently, it tends to insist that the defendant should be able to identify the class of people likely to rely on the information or service, and how such people are likely to rely on it.[7] General information made widely available is far more unlikely to attract a duty in tort law than information tailored to an individual's needs. This raises the interesting question of how a court would treat a non-human interactive advice-giving system. Because the experience of using such a system, for example, for medical

---

4 English tort law recognizes tort obligations arising between contracting parties before the conclusion of the contract (e.g. *Esso Petroleum Co Ltd* v. *Mardon* [1976] QB 801) and existing parallel to contractual obligations (e.g. *Henderson* v. *Merrett Syndicates Ltd* [1995] 2 AC 145).

5 *E.g. Williams* v. *Natural Life Health Foods Ltd* [1998] 1 WLR 830.

6 Under the Unfair Contract Terms Act 1977 where the defendant is a business and the task, if carelessly carried out, could lead to personal injury or property damage, any attempt to exclude liability will be ineffective. Where the task, if carelessly carried out, is only likely to cause financial loss then attempts to exclude liability will be assessed for 'reasonableness'. Relevant factors in determining 'reasonableness' will include the ease with which the duty to take reasonable care could have been satisfied, the likely burden of potential liability, and the practicality of absorbing such a burden through insurance or price rises (self-insurance).

7 E.g. *Caparo Industries Plc* v. *Dickman* [1990] 2 AC 605.

diagnosis[8] or for a minor legal problem,[9] is far closer to the experience of attending a doctor's surgery or solicitor's office than the experience of reading a medical encyclopaedia or legal self-help guide it is possible that courts will treat such a system as a doctor (attracting a duty to the user) rather than as a book (not attracting such a duty[10]). The more interactive and individualised the system, the more likely that there will be potential liability in tort for negligent advice.

Dependence/expertise. The greater the difference between the expertise that the defendant claims in the subject-matter and the expected level of competence of the reasonable consumer[11] in dealing with the subject matter, the more likely that an 'assumption of responsibility' will be found. In the context of on-line interactions three factors may be of particular importance. First, it will often be far easier for a non-expert to enter an electronic market for expertise than to enter a similar non-electronic market. This assertion can be loosely defended by consideration of the relative costs of setting up an office where advice is offered in person to clients attracted to the office, publishing and distributing a book offering advice, and publishing and distributing advice on a website.[12] With regard to books, the need (in most cases) to rely on a publisher's assistance to secure widespread exposure ensures that a third party (the publisher) often plays a quality-based gate-keeping function, at least to some degree. The same is not generally the case when a person publishes advice electronically. The low cost of publishing advice on-line may lead to both wider availability of 'low-quality' expertise and new availability of 'low-value' expertise.[13] Second, widely understood 'signals' of the reliability of expertise may not have developed yet in electronic markets for expertise.[14] Thus, so far as different publishers of books operate different levels of quality control many consumers may have some awareness of which publishers are most scrupulous. It is unclear that there exists an electronic equivalent of 'trusted publishers' or even an on-line equivalent of the certificates on

---

8 Such a system can be experienced at: <www.nhsdirect.nhs.uk/SelfHelp/index.asp>

9 Such a system can be experienced at: <www.freelawyer.co.uk>

10 Most attempts to claim for injuries suffered as a result of the carelessly-inaccurate contents of a book have been aimed at publishers rather than authors. Judgments in claims aimed at publishers have consistently denied a duty of care owed to readers, and some have expressly doubted whether authors owe such duties: *Demuth Development Corp* v. *Merck & Co* 432 F Supp 990 (USDC, 1977); *Jones* v. *J B Lippincott* 694 F Supp 1216 (D Md, 1988); *Winter* v. *G P Putnam's Sons* 938 F 2d 1033 (9th Cir, 1991).

11 The word 'consumer' is used throughout this section in a broad sense. Most of the points made apply to both individuals and businesses relying on the expertise of others.

12 The point made here is not that e-businesses are cheap to set up and operate. Recent history confirms the high cost of starting on-line retailing businesses. Rather the point is that it is relatively cheap to publish expert information, downloadable forms, and the like, on the Internet.

13 'Low value expertise' is intended to connote the phenomenon of 'expertise' which is not worth as much to a consumer as the cost of a book (still less, a live consultation with a professional) but is worth the lower effort involved in searching for a free website.

14 This is not to say that there have been no attempts to address this problem, merely that these attempts are not commonly known about. Many trade associations have codes of conduct covering Internet trading, and there have also been more general initiatives (e.g. the 'seal' available to sites signing up to the Internet Content Register's 'Internet Code of Practice', <www.internet.org.uk/icop.html>).

a professional's office walls, particularly not in the sector of 'low-value expertise'. Third, electronic contact may deprive consumers of some of the techniques commonly used to check expertise in face-to-face or telephone-based contact. For instance, it may be difficult to ask an on-line expert questions because the website format controls the sort of communications which are permitted. Further, the fact that on-line experts need not be locally based may reduce the likelihood that friends, neighbours and associates of the consumer will have had experiences of the same on-line expert which can be shared. Although it is, of course, likely that new 'signals' and 'check techniques' will develop reasonably rapidly it may be difficult for consumers to protect themselves against incompetent on-line expertise during the transition.[15] This may encourage courts to put aside any concerns about the risk of 'widespread liability' when developing tort law to protect consumers who make use of on-line 'expertise'.

Payment. An important role for the 'assumption of responsibility' doctrine in English law has been to create liabilities even where there has been no direct payment from consumer to expert. That said, the doctrine is generally not invoked where the defendant expert acted altruistically, or where the consumer is unreasonably seeking to 'free-ride' on a service being paid for by others. Thus the doctrine may be particularly applicable where the defendant provides the information or service in order to earn revenue from those who would like to advertise to consumers, or because the defendant wishes to attract the client into later forming some other relationship where there will be direct payment. Moreover, the more reasonable it might have been for the consumer to have contracted with an expert directly for a comparable service the less likely that a court will conclude that an unpaid expert was subject to a tort obligation. This will mean that providers of free advice and services will be more likely to owe duties where the expected class of consumers was known to be unlikely to consider it reasonable to pay for further advice on the same topic.[16]

Importance of the client's interests. The English courts will more readily find duties to take reasonable care to protect against personal injury or physical damage to existing property than to protect against pure economic losses. Thus websites offering medical diagnosis or advice on how to undertake potentially dangerous activities[17] will be more likely to attract liability than websites offering legal or investment advice. But even within the category of pure economic losses it seems that the English courts are willing to distinguish between types of losses on the basis of social importance (e.g. money invested in domestic houses, money passing under wills, increases in

---

15 The 'general information to be provided' under Article 5 of Directive 2000/31/EC will not go far towards offering protection against shoddy on-line expertise, though it will facilitate the enforcement of any rights created by the common law. This provision of the Directive was implemented in the United Kingdom by regulation 6 of The Electronic Commerce (EC Directive) Regulations 2002 (SI 2002 No 2013).

16 This will often be the case if the class is known to be financially hard-pressed, or if it is known that the class considers that it is already paying ('indirectly') for the free advice or service.

17 For instance, how to repair a car's brakes, how to service electrical equipment, or how to distinguish between venomous and non-venomous snakes.

prospective earnings through educational achievement *seem* to attract better protection than prospective profits of commercial investment[18]).

Conclusions on torts in situations akin to contract. The Internet offers a great advantage to consumers in the form of access to more information, more cheaply. It may also, however, reduce the capacity of consumers to protect themselves against poor quality expertise. Further, so far as the information is often provided to wide audiences (although sometimes tailored so as to appear individualised) and for payment which is indirect (e.g. advertising) courts will have to be careful not to create wide or overwhelming liabilities. The balance between the benefits of easy access to information and the need to protect vulnerable consumers will be difficult for courts to perfect, and they will not have the re-assurance that other parties, for instance publishers, are reliably investing in protecting consumers.

3 Defective e-products

The issue for consideration under this sub-heading is that which will arise where the claimant is harmed by an electronic 'product', for instance, a programme that has been downloaded. Where the claimant purchased[19] the 'product' and wishes to sue the vendor the matter will, in England, be governed by contract law. Where the claimant was not a purchaser,[20] or was a purchaser but wishes to sue the producer of the 'product' rather than the vendor, then the matter will, in England, proceed under the law of tort.[21] There may be a subdivision, however, depending on whether the harm suffered is personal injury, damage to property intended for private use and so used, or damage to property not intended for private use or not so used. Only personal injury and damage to private use property can ever fall under the special statutory tort regime for defective products, the Consumer Protection Act 1987,[22] whilst business use property will have to be sued for in the tort of negligence.[23] Importantly, where the claim falls under the Act all attempts to exclude the liability by contract

---

18 The relevant cases are: *Smith* v. *Eric S Bush* [1990] 1 AC 831 (domestic house); *White* v. *Jones* [1995] 2 AC 207 (will); *Phelps* v. *Hillingdon LBC* [2001] 2 AC 619 (education); *Caparo Industries plc* v. *Dickman* [1990] 2 AC 605 (commercial investment).

19 Or licensed, or hired, etc.. Throughout this paragraph references to 'purchase' should be taken also to include contracts other than sale-purchase.

20 This will be the case where the programme was supplied to the claimant directly but without payment, or indirectly (e.g. through a friend or relation), or even if it was never supplied to the claimant (e.g. virus supplied to another infects the claimant's computer).

21 Technically speaking, although the regime imposed by the Consumer Protection Act 1987 is non-contractual it is also difficult to classify as part of the law of tort. This is because it is not a condition of a successful claim that the claimant must demonstrate wrongful behaviour by the defendant. Nonetheless, the topic is commonly discussed in textbooks on the law of tort.

22 The Consumer Protection Act 1987 is the United Kingdom's attempt to implement the EC Directive on Defective Products (No 85/374/EEC).

23 The relevant provision is s 5(3) Consumer Protection Act 1987.

will be ineffective,[24] whilst such attempts *may* be successful against common law negligence claims.[25]

But can a downloaded computer programme[26] fall within the special regime for defective products at all?[27] Consider, for example, a downloaded guide to rock-climbing routes which misdirects me up a very perilous ascent where I am injured, and a downloaded kitchen-design programme which is contaminated with a virus which damages my computer. The Consumer Protection Act 1987, s. 1(2) assists with this question only to the extent that it defines 'product' as meaning 'any goods or electricity'. Similarly, Article 2 of the Product Liability Directive states 'all moveables' and 'electricity'.[28] Before close scrutiny of these provisions it may be helpful to summarize the position in the United States of America.

In the United States of America, before the Third Restatement of Torts in 1998, most courts had already reached the conclusion that the 'paper and print' of books could be products but that ideas and expression thereof were not: *Winter* v. *G P Putnam's Sons*.[29] Consequently, the courts did not treat 'a book' as a single composite product, but as separably 'paper and print' (a product) and 'information' (not a product). The view that 'information' fell outside the scope of product liability has been expressly extended to the contents of violent and pornographic video-games, movies, and website materials.[30] But although 'information' was generally not treated as a product, even if supplied on a tangible medium, a peculiar exception was maintained for maps and navigation charts. These were treated as products, principally on the basis of a supposed analogy with a defective compass. Moreover, in *Winter* the court suggested that this exception might also cover defective software.

The Third Restatement of Torts: Product Liability (1998), § 19 employs a focal definition of 'product' as 'tangible personal property' but extends this by stating that 'other items ... are products when the context of their distribution and use is sufficiently analogous to the distribution and use of tangible personal property that it is appropriate to apply the rules stated in this Restatement.' Comment d. to this provision indicates that this definition was intended to preserve the *Winter* position ('information' not a product), and also expresses support for ceasing to treat maps and

---

24 Section 7; Article 12.

25 Unfair Contract Terms Act 1977; Unfair Terms in Consumer Contract Regulations 1999.

26 The question of what might count as a 'downloaded computer programme' will not be discussed. It seems clear, however, that 'applet objects' fall within this phrase.

27 The question whether software is a 'product' within the Consumer Protection Act 1987 is one of the matters dealt with by Professor Jane Stapleton in 'Software, Information and the Concept of Product', *Tel Aviv University Studies in Law* 9 (1989) p. 147. In 1989, however, the state of technological development meant that the issue of 'downloading' was understandably undiscussed.

28 The question whether a downloaded programme might be 'electricity' will not be considered in detail. Any attempt to classify such a programme as a 'product' on the basis that it is *transferred* as 'electricity' would risk converting a wide range of other things into 'products'. For instance, the information I gave to X on the telephone was transferred as electricity, but surely we would not want such information to count as a 'product' if communicated on the telephone whilst not a 'product' if communicated in person.

29 *Winter* v. *G P Putnam's Sons* 938 F 2d 1033 (9th Cir. 1991) (Encyclopaedia of Mushrooms, advice in it causing severe liver damage).

30 *James* v. *Meow Media and others* 300 F 3d 683 (6th Cir. 2002).

charts as products. The comment is neutral, however, on the specific question whether software should be considered a product. The Reporters suggest in a note that courts faced with this decision may choose to rely on cases under the Uniform Commercial Code which have distinguished between off-the-shelf software, held to be 'goods', and specially written software, held to be a 'service'. To a significant extent, however, this distinction ignores the realities of computer programming, where the concept of a programme written from a blank-sheet (blank-screen?) is a rarity, and many specially-written programmes are actually tailored composites of pre-written code. Further, even if this distinction seems sensible when one is considering liability for failure to perform intended function (e.g. it does not safely guide you up the rock face) it is harder to understand why the off-the-shelf / made-to-measure distinction should be crucial in cases of contamination with a virus.[31]

Interestingly, contamination may best be considered a 'manufacturing error', thus potentially attracting strict liability under the Third Restatement, whilst failure to perform intended function is more likely to be a 'design error'. Consequently, with the Third Restatement's re-assertion of a fault-based standard for design errors it may make little difference to 'function failure' cases whether they fall within products liability or negligence. It may, however, make a considerable difference in 'manufacturing error' cases.

Returning to the position in the United Kingdom, the 1987 Act clearly invites reference to legal definitions of 'goods'. But the Sale of Goods Act 1979, s. 61,[32] offers only a non-exhaustive definition of this term, stating that 'goods' 'includes all personal chattels other than things in action and money'. Interpreting this provision in *St Albans City and District Council* v. *International Computers Ltd*,[33] Sir Iain Glidewell offered the opinion that a tangible disk was clearly within the definition and a computer programme of itself was not, and, more importantly, that supply of a programme on a tangible disk would be treated as the supply of composite 'goods', not the separate supply of a disk (goods) and a programme (not goods).[34] He drew no distinction between different types of software, for instance between software which principally delivers information (and would be excluded from the reach of product liability under *Winter*) and software which performs tasks, or functions like a tool. If the Glidewell approach was applied to s 1(2) of the Consumer Protection Act 1987 then the producer of software on disks would potentially be subject to wider tort lia-

31 Similarly, the distinction seems less attractive in cases where the person injured may not be the person who made an election between off-the-shelf and tailor-made.

32 The same definition is used by the Supply of Goods and Services Act 1982, s. 18.

33 *St Albans City and District Council* v. *International Computers Ltd* [1996] 4 All ER 481, at 492-3.

34 This has generated further case law on whether the composite 'goods' are supplied when the programme-carrying disk is taken to the customer's premises, the programme is loaded onto the customer's hardware, and the programme-carrying disk is then taken away. It has been suggested that this procedure involves a bailment of the composite 'goods' into which terms of merchantability and fitness for purpose can be implied: *Watford Electronics Ltd* v. *Sanderson CFL Ltd* [2001] IP & T 148 (Technology and Construction Court, 27 July 2000). If so, it may also be a 'supply' of the 'product' so that the defence in s. 4(1)(b) of the Consumer Protection Act 1987 is inapplicable. This defence is of some importance since without it downloaded programmes might fall within the Act simply because they were held as composite products (i.e. within or on tangibles such as disks) by the supplier before being downloaded.

bility than the producer of downloadable software. Moreover, the producer of information distributed on a disk might be subject to a wider liability than the producer of information distributed orally.[35] Although these conclusions may appear surprising, they are in fact consistent with other better known examples of the incoherence of the product / services distinction. Professor Stapleton, for instance, has pointed to the fact that pharmaceuticals supplied in packaging which gives incorrect instructions about safe use are likely to be treated as a composite 'product' subject to the strict statutory regime, whilst a pharmacist giving identical instructions orally in response to an inquiry would only be subject to liability for 'negligent service'.[36] Similarly, to reject the disk / download distinction may only be to shift the position of an incoherent distinction, not to reject it outright. This is because it is widely accepted that a car or washing-machine can be a defective product within the statutory regime even if the lack of safety is attributable to an error in the software controlling a computerized component.[37]

Given that s 1(2) does not expressly incorporate the definition of 'goods' from s 61 of the Sale of Goods Act 1979 it remains possible that an English court may decide that the word 'goods' has different meanings in the two statutes. Such a decision would allow the court to conclude (i) that software on a disc is not always a composite product within the scope of the 1987 Act, and (ii) that software not on a disc is not necessarily outside the scope of the 1987 Act. The main support for these two propositions, as the Reporters for the Third Restatement suggest, comes from the fact that the policy reasons for a special regime of products liability apply reasonably strongly to the producers of off-the-shelf task-performing software, but (a) far less strongly to information-delivering software, and (b) as strongly to task-performing software whether it is supplied on a disc or downloaded. A further argument for extending the scope of products liability to task-performing software even if not supplied on disc would be that a narrow reading of the scope of the 1979 Act can often be cured by implying comparable terms into the contract at common law, whilst, by contrast, a narrow reading of the scope of the 1987 Act would leave injured consumers to the unsatisfactory vagaries of the tort of negligence. A judge willing to resist the lure of a simple equation with s 61, might reach conclusions consistent with (i) and (ii) by drawing on § 19 and holding that 'goods' in s 1(2) means 'all things, including intangible things, when the context of their distribution and use is sufficiently analogous to the distribution and use of tangible goods that it is appropriate to apply the rules in Part 1 of the 1987 Act'. Of course, this approach will not solve all problems. In particular, as previously mentioned, the distinction between information-delivering and task-performing software loses its attraction when the form that the 'defect' takes is contamination with a virus.

---

35 Other startling consequences might also follow by analogy with Sir Iain Glidewell's 'composite product' reasoning. For instance, would a book be treated as a composite product so as to create possible liability under the Consumer Protection Act 1987 for a defect in the information in it?

36 Stapleton 1989, p 149 (see note 27).

37 To put the same point in other words: If software supplied in a car is treated as part of a composite product then the law has already accepted that software can be 'productized' by 'absorption' into a physical medium. Consequently, the issue is merely one about where to draw the line between when software has been 'productized' in this way and when not.

To summarize, there is currently uncertainty as to the legal regime applicable to the producers and distributors of defective software, at least so far as that software causes damage to persons other than those in contractual privity with their preferred defendant. The uncertainty flows from use of the word 'goods' in the 1987 Act, and from the wide range of 'things' covered by the single word 'software'. Thus the range stretches from 'things' which are indistinguishable from 'information', through 'things' which look analogous to tools, on to 'things' which seem to perform individual 'services'. Whilst the temptation to treat 'goods' as having the same meaning as in s 61 of the Sale of Goods Act 1979 will be strong, and the principal deleterious result of equation will merely be to add further examples to the existing list of examples of incoherence at the borderline between products and services, there is at least some scope for adopting a definition of 'goods' more closely tailored to the policy which underpins the 1987 Act.

4 Torts involving culpable encouragement of wrongdoing by others and culpable failure to control others

English law does not recognize any general private law duty to prevent wrongdoing by others. Instead it identifies situations where a person may be jointly liable with another, and special categories of situation where a duty to take reasonable steps to prevent wrongdoing by another may arise.[38] As will become apparent, these two bases for liability tend to shade into one another.

Joint liability: Incitement. The most relevant ground for holding a provider of web facilities[39] jointly liable for a tort committed by a third party may be incitement. It seems to be accepted that a defendant can be held liable for inciting another to commit a tort even though there is no civil liability for 'aiding and abetting' another's tort.[40] But to be held liable for inciting another to commit a tort it seems that a defendant must 'share a common design' with that other that actions amounting to the tort should be done.[41] Incitement does not, however, require express verbal agreement or active encouragement, and can be committed by the provision of equipment necessary for committing a wrong. Indeed, in a state with strong free speech guarantees it may be more difficult to impose liability for 'incitement' wholly contained in words

38 One well-known category is where an occupier of land is aware that a third party is using the land in such a way as to endanger or annoy neighbours, e.g. *Lippiatt* v. *South Gloucestershire CC* [2000] QB 51.

39 There may be two different types of behaviour worth considering (beyond straightforward examples of incitement): First, where the defendant supplies 'know-how', for instance, instructions on how to build pipe bombs, and second, where the defendant supplies 'easy opportunity', for instance a chat room where those inclined to exchange confidential price-sensitive information can do so anonymously.

40 *Credit Lyonnais Bank Nederland NV* v. *Export Credits Guarantee Department* [2000] 1 AC 486. The topic is discussed in more detail in the Court of Appeal, [1998] 1 Lloyd's Rep 19.

41 *CBS Songs Ltd* v. *Amstrad Consumer Electronics plc* [1988] AC 1013, at 1058, *per* Lord Templeman.

than for 'incitement' involving provision of necessary equipment.[42] But in England merely providing necessary equipment is unlikely to be sufficient in itself if the equipment potentially has lawful uses. Thus in *CBS Songs Ltd* v. *Amstrad Consumer Electronics plc,*[43] which concerned whether the manufacturers of twin-deck tape-recording machines could be held responsible for infringements of copyright by those who copied music cassettes, the House of Lords held that the manufacturers did not incite pirate copying. In reaching this conclusion Lord Templeman was apparently influenced by the fact that the machines could be used for lawful purposes, and Amstrad did not seek to procure any particular infringer to commit any particular infringement.

A different result may be reached, however, where the defendant does not supply the necessary equipment once and for all by sale but instead continues to provide access to the necessary equipment, even after becoming aware that it is being used to commit wrongs.[44] Continuing to provide access in such circumstances may make it difficult for courts to resist the inference of a 'common design'.

Creation or supply of dangerous matter: It seems, however, that there is a possible basis for liability broader than this narrow concept of incitement which applies where the defendant has created or supplied potentially dangerous matter.[45] This basis is most clearly recognized in cases where the 'matter' is made available to children. Thus there is a group of cases in English law holding liable those who make accessible to children 'matter' that they are likely to misuse and cause injury with, if they do misuse it and cause injury.[46] These cases could form a foundation for the claim that the developer of, for instance, a computer virus should be liable if he failed to take reasonable steps to prevent it from becoming accessible to children who might predictably misuse it. In *Smith* v. *Littlewoods Organization Ltd*[47] Lord Goff generalizes such cases as involving the defendant's failure to control a source of danger that he

---

42 An example of the difficulties is provided by the case of *Planned Parenthood of Columbia/Willamette, Inc* v. *American Coalition of Life Activists* 290 F 3d 1058 (9th Cir. 2002). This case considered whether publication on the worldwide web of 'wanted posters' of doctors working in abortion clinics, including their addresses, was protected by the First Amendment or was an unprotected threat.

43 *CBS Songs Ltd* v. *Amstrad Consumer Electronics plc* [1988] AC 1013.

44 This seems to have supplied one of the bases for liability in the Napster litigation: *A&M Records Inc* v. *Napster Inc* 239 F.3d 1004 (9th Cir, 2001), at 1021, 'We agree that if a computer system operator learns of specific infringing material available on his system and fails to purge such material from the system, the operator knows of and contributes to direct infringement. Conversely, absent any specific information which identifies infringing activity, a computer system operator cannot be liable for contributory infringement merely because the structure of the system allows for the exchange of copyrighted material' (footnote omitted). There are also signs, however, that the principles governing secondary and vicarious liability for copyright infringement in the United States are not identical to the principles governing secondary and vicarious liability for other civil wrongs.

45 In this section it is assumed that this 'matter' is held not to be a 'defective product' within the scope of the Consumer Protection Act 1987.

46 Many of the cases involve guns, but the principle is broader. See e.g. *Williams* v. *Eady* (1893) 10 TLR 41 (jar of phosphorus); *Jackson* v. *London CC* (1912) 28 TLR 359 (building material in school playground). Whether the principle can ever cover misuse by adults is discussed below.

47 *Smith* v. *Littlewoods Organization Ltd.* [1987] AC 241.

is responsible for. In formulating the general principle Lord Goff did not exclude the possibility that such a duty could extend to include potential liability for failing to control adults. All the examples, hypothetical and real, that he gave, however, involved children. Similarly, in the earlier case of *P Perl (Exporters) Ltd* v. *Camden LBC*,[48] as Robert Goff LJ, he suggested that the principle might cover situations where an adult was known to be drunk or incompetent. This might provide a foundation for imposing a duty to take care not to supply dangerous matter to 'adults known to be incapable of resisting the temptation to misuse it'.

In the United States of America most of the courts which have refused to hold that books, video-games and websites are products have also held that, in the absence of incitement, creators are not liable for failing to anticipate and guard against criminal acts inspired or otherwise facilitated by their creations even when the criminal actors were children.[49] But an example of a case falling on the other side of the line may be provided by *Weirum* v. *RKO*.[50] In this case the court was willing to hold a radio station liable for an accident caused by listeners driving negligently whilst trying to catch up with a lure. This suggests that the degree of foreseeability of the dangerous behaviour of the third party using the defendant's dangerous 'matter' may be crucial.

Applying the principles developed above it is possible to predict that courts will attach liability to 'common design' incitement and the creation of matter that is highly likely to be used dangerously, but will not impose liability on other forms of facilitation of wrongdoing, particularly if the facilities provided may be used in lawful ways. If *Weirum* is a reliable precedent then companies providing the framework for games played by action in public using hand-held computers may have to be careful to avoid liability.[51] But the provision of facilities for sending anonymous e-mail or for publishing messages anonymously, is likely to be insufficient to attract liability: Such facilities appear to have a legitimate purpose and consequently are likely to be treated like the twin-deck tape-recorder.[52]

---

48 *P Perl (Exporters) Ltd* v. *Camden LBC* [1984] QB 342, at 359. The Court of Appeal considered this suggestion in *Topp* v. *London Country Bus (South West) Ltd* [1993] 1 WLR 976, where the claimant had been injured by a bus taken by an unknown person from a lay-by next to public house where the defendant had left it unlocked and with the key in the ignition. The Court held, however, that the case was distinguishable from Robert Goff LJ's hypothetical since there was no evidence that the unknown person had come from the public house.

49 E.g. *James* v. *Meow Media and others* 300 F 3d. 683 (6th Cir. 2002) (in this case it was suggested that a teenager had been inspired to shoot three people by exposure to violent video games and movies, and the games and movies had also desensitized him to the extent necessary for him to be willing to indulge in such violence).

50 *Weirum* v. *RKO* 539 P 2d 36 (1975).

51 Several games involving use of mobile phones give benefits to players who get within a certain distance of other players. This will obviously encourage 'chasing'. It seems possible that any attempt to avoid liability by compelling players to promise that they will observe safety rules will be ineffective if it is foreseeable that the excitement of the competition will lead to widespread flouting of such rules.

52 Of course if the provider of the facility in some way actively encouraged the posting of, for instance, confidential documents, it may become liable through 'incitement'.

Defamation and Internet service providers: The discussion so far is probably sufficient to answer how far Internet service providers can be held liable for failing to prevent or limit the commission by others of wrongs such as deceit, copyright infringement, violation of privacy, and knowing infliction of psychiatric distress. English law, however, does not categorise cases involving providing facilities for defamation as cases of failure to control third parties. Instead, because the English tort of defamation has a broad definition of 'publication' and an easily satisfied mental element, printers, distributors and sellers of written material can be jointly liable with the author for defamation. Thus innocent transmitters of defamatory material are held liable for 'publishing' that material unless they can establish the defence of 'innocent dissemination',[53] or its contemporary supplement, the statutory defence found in s 1 of the Defamation Act 1996. It seems likely that these rules mean that most parties involved in the production of websites will be publishers, and will bear the burden of establishing a defence to avoid liability for defamatory material on those websites. Indeed, the creator of a website containing a hyperlink to another site containing defamatory material is likely to be held to be a publisher of that material so far as browsers follow the link.[54]

This law was applied to the situation of an anonymous posting to a newsgroup stored on the defendant Internet service provider's server in *Godfrey* v. *Demon Internet Ltd*.[55] In this case Morland J held that every time a customer accessed the posting the defendant was responsible for a publication to that customer.[56] He then went on to consider the applicability of the s 1 defence, but found that the defendant had failed to establish this because it continued to publish the posting after it had reason to believe that it was contributing to the publication of a defamatory statement.[57]

The question arises how far English law has been changed by implementation Directive 2000/31/EC.[58] The European Community took an interest in the liability of Internet service providers in the interest of fostering e-commerce in Europe and ensuring that Internet service providers and others do not migrate to jurisdictions with

53 Thus booksellers and libraries might be obliged to establish the defence of 'innocent dissemination' in order to avoid liability for publishing defamatory statements contained in the books that they sold or lent: *Weldon* v. *Times Book Co. Ltd.* [1911] 28 *TLR* 143; *Vizetelly* v. *Mudie's Select Library* [1900] 2 QB 170.

54 M Collins, *The Law of Defamation and the Internet* (Oxford University Press, Oxford, 2001), paragraph 5.30. Such a principle could cause significant problems for search engines.

55 *Godfrey* v. *Demon Internet Ltd* [2001] QB 201, [1999] 4 All ER 342.

56 The Court of Appeal has recently confirmed that there is a fresh publication (and hence a fresh limitation period begins to run) every time information on a website is accessed: *Loutchansky* v. *Times Newspapers Ltd (No. 2)* [2002] 1 All ER 652.

57 The victim of the defamation claimed to have faxed the defendant's managing director informing him that the posting was a forgery on 17 January, but the posting remained available on the news server until 27 January.

58 Directive 2000/31/EC of the European Parliament and of the Council of 8 June 2000 on certain legal aspects of information society services, in particular electronic commerce, in the Internal Market (Directive on electronic commerce). The Directive has been implemented in the United Kingdom by The Electronic Commerce (EC Directive) Regulations 2002 (SI 2002 No 2013) [hereafter 'the Regulations']. But the discussion that follows refers to the provisions of the Directive since they will guide interpretation of the Regulations.

more protective liability regimes.[59] Chapter II, Section 4 (Articles 12-15) of the Directive deals with both criminal and civil liability of providers of such services. Indeed, only Article 14[60] draws any distinction between criminal prosecutions and claims for damages. All the provisions, however, distinguish between liability and the possibility of being required by judicial or executive order to take steps to terminate or prevent an infringement. Thus whilst Chapter II, Section 4 grants various intermediary service providers extensive immunities from liability it does not preclude them from being compelled to co-operate in removing illegal information or disabling access to it.

The Directive insists on different levels of immunity for those who take on different roles in access to Internet content. Article 12 of the Directive covers those whose role is limited to being 'mere conduits'. It provides that Member States must ensure that an information society service provider which merely transmits information or provides access is not liable for the information transmitted. This immunity is conditional on the provider (a) not initiating the transmission, (b) not selecting the receiver of the transmission, and (c) not selecting or modifying the information. Paragraph (43) of the preamble clarifies that 'manipulations of a technical nature which take place in the course of the transmission' will not count as 'modifications' provided that they 'do not alter the integrity of the information'.[61] Article 13 provides a similar immunity for service providers which merely 'cache' information.

Article 14 provides an immunity for 'hosting' information. Thus this will be the most relevant provision for those providing facilities such as those considered in *Godfrey*. A facility provider ceases to be protected if it is not merely a 'host' but has authority or control over the provider of the information that is 'hosted'.[62] Experience from the United States of America suggests that this borderline will be hotly disputed. In the United States, before the 1996 statute, some bulletin board 'hosts' found that they were paradoxically subjected to more stringent liability rules if they maintained some degree of control over content, and hence became 'publisher-editors', rather than leaving it wholly supervised and remaining mere 'distributors'.[63] Indeed, the breadth of the immunity for 'hosts' and 'editors' in the 1996 statute was largely prompted by a desire to encourage such self-policing.[64]

---

59 The United States of America has a very protective regime in 47 USC s 230(c) (The Communications Decency Act 1996).

60 Concerning 'hosting'. The same distinction is transposed into regulation 19 of the Regulations.

61 The United Kingdom Government's consultation on implementation of the Directive revealed that there are likely to be difficult questions about the definition of 'modify'.

62 Article 14(2).

63 A notorious example of this was *Stratton Oakmount Inc* v. *Prodigy Services Co* 23 Media L Rep 1794 (NY Sup Ct, 1995).

64 The result of the statutory immunity may have been to save principled service providers from an unfairness in the law by creating a new unfairness in the law for the victims of unprincipled service providers: *Blumenthal* v. *Drudge* 992 F Supp 44 (DDC, 1998), 'Congress has conferred immunity from tort liability as an incentive to Internet service providers to self-police the Internet for obscenity and other offensive material, even where the self-policing is unsuccessful or not even attempted'.

The Article 14 immunity is made conditional on an absence of actual knowledge of illegal activity or information, and, as regards claims for damages, an absence of awareness of facts or circumstances from which the illegal activity or information is apparent, or expeditious action on obtaining such knowledge or awareness. This provision must be read alongside article 15 and paragraph (48) of the preamble. Article 15 insists that 'Member States shall not impose a general obligation on providers, when providing the services covered by Articles 12, 13 and 14, to monitor the information which they transmit or store, nor a general obligation actively to seek facts or circumstances indicating illegal activity.' Paragraph (48) states, however, that 'This Directive does not affect the possibility for Member States of requiring service providers, who 'host' information provided by recipients of their service, to apply duties of care, which can reasonably be expected from them and which are specified by national law, in order to detect and prevent certain types of illegal activities.'

It takes some ingenuity to reconcile these propositions relating to 'hosts'. The greatest tension comes from the fact that Article 14 envisages no liability without actual awareness of facts, which tends to be supported by Article 15's insistence of no general duty actively to seek facts, whilst paragraph 48 envisages the possibility of 'duties of care ... in order to detect and prevent.' The problem with this is that a duty to detect illegality makes little sense unless it *precedes* awareness of facts which already make illegality apparent. But consequently it is difficult to understand a duty to detect which is not a duty to seek facts. Perhaps the answer to the difficulty is that in specific circumstances (i.e. not generally) Member States can impose a duty to seek facts in order to detect illegality (thus avoiding Article 15's prohibition). But here we run into the problem that it is not clear what the remedy for a breach of the specific-circumstances duty would be because under Article 14 there can be no liability unless the provider has reached actual awareness.[65]

A further uncertainty stems from Article 14's failure to make clear whether the 'host' must be aware of sufficient facts to make a claim of unlawful activity arguable, or sufficient facts to be clear that no defence to such a claim exists.[66] Some idea of the practical problems which might be caused by the drafting of Article 14 can be glimpsed by taking the example of the provider who 'hosts' a site which displays an anonymous posting accusing Professor Website of plagiarism and shoddy scholarship. Such a posting (in English law) is obviously sufficient to make a *claim* against the author arguable (there is publication by the author and the assertion is defamatory). But the claim will only succeed if the assertion is one of fact and is untrue (i.e. the author fails to establish the defence of justification), or is one of opinion and is beyond the scope of reasonable opinion on a matter of public interest (i.e. the author fails to establish the defence of fair comment). Professor Website complains to the 'host' that

65 One possibility might be that the specific-circumstances duty could only be imposed by a judicial order, and consequently breach would be a contempt of court. A contempt might be punishable despite Article 14 because this Article only prohibits 'liability for the information stored' rather than liability for failing to comply with a judicial order.

66 There are, of course, a range of other possibilities. Some of those who responded to the United Kingdom Government's consultation on implementation recommended making pivotal the receipt of a notice setting out the alleged illegality with a formal claim that the notice was issued in good faith and was accurate.

the posting is defamatory. At this stage the 'host' should have knowledge of facts from which it is apparent that a wrong *may* have been committed, but is not yet in any position to judge whether the assertion of fact is untrue or the opinion wholly unreasonable. Article 14(1)(a) suggests that it is 'illegality' which must be apparent, and if this is taken to include that it must be apparent that 'all possible defences will fail' then it is difficult to understand how the 'host' will reach this state without a duty to take reasonable care to investigate further. But, as stated above, the duty mentioned in paragraph 48 does not explicitly appear in Articles 14 or 15, and in the face of Article 14's immunity it is not clear what the remedy for breach of such a duty might be.[67]

Whilst it is not possible to offer a conclusive answer on the width of the immunities from the Directive until the drafting problems are resolved it already seems certain that the immunity for 'hosts' will be broader than the defence in s 1 of the Defamation Act 1996. It will not, however, be as broad as the comparable immunity in the law of the United States, since this protects a wider range of 'hosts'.[68]

A further interesting contrast between the Directive and US Code, Title 47, Section 230 is that the latter seeks to provide an immunity for acts done in good faith by service providers to restrict further access to or availability of material that is 'harassing or otherwise objectionable'. Without such an immunity a service provider may risk litigation if it takes steps, for instance, to remove an offending message from a bulletin board. Indeed, acts such as these may themselves be defamatory! With such an immunity, however, service providers may have an incentive to over-react and to censor ('voluntarily') to a greater extent than legal restraints on free speech require.

It is not possible to offer a definitive answer to the question whether Internet service providers *should* be granted the broad immunities found in Section 230 and the EC Directive.[69] To an extent their self-portrayed image as public beneficiaries providing free or cheap access to an incredibly useful service, and as innocent conduits equivalent to telephone service providers, is persuasive.[70] Against this, however, must be balanced the image of the service providers, particularly 'hosts', as providing (and encouraging) access to a new form of social space, that form of space being one where wide publication is cheap, anonymous interaction is facilitated, self-pro-

---

67 The position may be complicated further in the United Kingdom by the fact that the Government chose not to transpose Article 15 (the requirement not to impose a general obligation to monitor) into the Regulations. The Government's response to public consultation (31 July 2002) claimed that this was because transposition of Article 15 would not confer any additional legal certainty and 'could even introduce uncertainty if the prohibition were interpreted differently from its meaning in the Directive'. This seems to suggest that the Government believes that reference to Article 15 is not necessary in order to interpret Article 14.

68 It is argued above that 'hosts' who are involved with the production of content will, because of Article 14(2), fall outside the scope of the Article 14 immunity more easily than they will fall outside the scope of US Code, Title 47, S 230(c)(1).

69 The question whether the immunities are compatible with Article 6 of the European Convention on Human Rights will not be discussed here. Suffice it to say that given the uncertain current state of the law concerning what is a 'restriction on access to court', it is arguable that the immunity will only be compatible if its restriction of civil rights is proportionate to a legitimate aim.

70 The 'mere conduit' argument certainly seems strong when dealing with providers which are only involved with transmission. The Post Office in the United Kingdom enjoys statutory immunity: Postal Services Act 2000, s 90(1)(a).

tection is often impractical, and policing on behalf of the public is limited. The American immunities were created in order to promote self-policing by service providers. Thus the American legislators have engineered a trade-off between more protection against obscenity and other evils by 'good citizen' service providers in exchange for less protection for reputations from all service providers.[71] By contrast, the rhetoric used to justify the European immunity attaches more weight to reducing the impact of liability rules in order to facilitate the development of a nascent industry. This trade-off may well be economically justifiable in terms of the long-term creation of wealth in Europe, but it also has a distributive dimension: The fairness of this redistribution may depend on whether the persons who regret the diminution in protection for their reputations are approximately the same persons who are gaining from the development of the nascent industry. If there is no approximate identification then historians of twenty-first century tort history will find it far easier to prove a 'subsidy thesis' than historians of nineteenth-century tort law.[72]

5 Damaging an e-business

E-businesses, like other businesses, will be vulnerable to damage by defamation, malicious falsehood, deceit, passing off, and a host of specialized torts. The torts which may raise the most interesting questions, however, are likely to be the general torts – negligence, dealing with careless damage, and interference with trade by unlawful means, dealing with deliberate harm.

Negligence. If we take as a problem case the workman who carelessly severs a data cable, the analogy with careless damage to electricity cables may be apposite. In such cases English courts have famously distinguished between physical damage to property caused by interruptions of electricity supply, financial losses consequential on that physical damage, and pure economic loss from business interruption. Thus *Spartan Steel*[73] recovered compensation for the raw materials damaged when power to their smelter was cut off, and for the profits they would have made had they been able to process and sell those raw materials, but **not** for the profits they would have made had they been able to process four more batches whilst waiting for the power to be re-connected. Pure economic losses from business interruption are generally not recoverable in claims founded on the tort of negligence: A rule which is shared by most, but not all, states in the United States of America.[74]

---

71 It was America Online (AOL), which was the service provider relying on the statutory immunity to protect it from liability arising out of its relationship with Matt Drudge: *Blumenthal* v. *Drudge* 992 F Supp 44 (DDC, 1998).

72 The 'subsidy thesis' is commonly associated with Professor Morton J. Horwitz, *The Transformation of American Law 1780-1860* (Harvard University Press, Cambridge, 1977). It has been strongly criticized by, amongst others, G. T. Schwartz, 'Tort Law and the Economy in Nineteenth Century America: A Reinterpretation', Yale LJ 90 (1981) 1717.

73 *Spartan Steel & Alloys Ltd* v. *Martin & Co (Contractors) Ltd* [1973] QB 27.

74 See e.g. R. Rabin, 'Tort Recovery For Negligently Inflicted Economic Loss: A Reassessment', *Stanford Law Review* 37 (1985), 1513.

This rule makes the ownership of data cables important. Even an exclusive contractual right to use a cable will not, on current English authority, confer a right to sue for the cost of repair and economic losses pending repair.[75] But ownership will confer such a right.

A further important question will concern how 'data damage' is conceptualised. So far as damage to a cable (owned by a third party) leads to the 'loss', 'irrecoverability' or 'muddling' of data it will be important to determine whether such re-direction or re-organization of electrons is 'property damage' or merely 'economic loss'. The main argument against treating it as property damage is probably the lack of tangibility.[76] But it is submitted that there are stronger reasons from the perspective of policy for treating it as equivalent to property damage: In particular, that the loss is contained (not usually shared by a wide field of potential claimants[77]) and is a waste-loss (the data is genuinely lost/wasted, rather than being re-allocated[78]).

Interference with trade by unlawful means. This tort can protect a claimant against a defendant who aims at causing economic harm to him or her. Two categories of persons are commonly defendants: Commercial rivals of the claimant and persons who have a grievance against the claimant.[79] In cases where there seems no doubt that the required mental element[80] is established the central issue is likely to be whether the defendant made use of 'unlawful means' in pursuing its campaign. English law insists that the means must be shown to have been 'unlawful', not merely 'unjustifiable' or 'contrary to good business ethics'.[81]

Most cases involve unlawful means in the form of torts against third parties. Thus C can sue D for economic losses if D tortiously damaged the property of T with the aim of causing harm to C. An important question, however, is how the courts will deal

75 *Londonwaste Ltd* v. *Amec Civil Engineering Ltd* [1997] 53 Con LR 66, where the unsuccessful claimant had a contractual right to use the (electricity) cable, made exclusive use of it, and had even paid a sum towards its installation, but was still unsuccessful.

76 As discussed above, however, it is possible for courts to artificially convert 'data damage' into physical damage if the circumstances allow the 'data' to be treated as part of a composite product with the storage medium. Even this is probably impossible, however, if the damage is the 'loss' or 'muddling' of the data before it reached the storage medium.

77 One of the strongest policy justifications for the English 'bright line rule' against allowing recovery for negligently inflicted pure economic loss is the fear that such losses ripple (i.e. A's loss leads to further loss to B, leads to further loss to C, etc.) with the result that there may be an indeterminate number of claimants. The argument here is that drawing the line so that compensation for 'data damage' is recoverable will be drawing the line before the ripple starts.

78 In many cases involving lost profits 'lost to A' means 'obtained by B instead'. Awarding compensation to A in such cases might lead to particular industries being more profitable than they ought to be. Consequently, if (i) A is a long term participant in the industry, (ii) the particular loss is not so large as to be impossible to absorb, and (iii) over time A will as often be a beneficiary as a loser, then it may be more efficient (and not unjust) to refuse to compensate A.

79 This may cover, for instance, protest groups campaigning against a company's policies and disgruntled employees.

80 This is quite narrow; that 'the defendant was aiming at causing loss to the claimant'.

81 This insistence is attributed to the House of Lords' decision in *Allen* v. *Flood* [1898] AC 1. For a recent defence of this decision against alternative doctrines that are adopted in other European jurisdictions see T. Weir, *Economic Torts* (Clarendon Press, Oxford, 1997).

with a case where D is aiming at obtaining a competitive advantage over C and in pursuing this aim violates some regulation relating to, for instance, data use. Legal scholars have split on this issue. Some argue that everything that is unlawful under any body of applicable law should be capable of fulfilling the tort's requirement of 'unlawful means'.[82] This view has the great merit of simplicity.[83] Others argue, however, that the tort's purpose is to deal with forbidden methods of competition, and that some regulations make defined behaviour unlawful for reasons completely different from whether it should be a forbidden means in competition between D and C.[84] For instance, if D (a car producer) makes an advertisement pointing out the unreliability of C (another car producer)'s vehicles and in making the advertisement D unlawfully requires a child actor to be on the set for longer than the regulations permitting exceptional working by young children allow, the second group would argue that this should not make the situation one where loss has been caused by unlawful means. The regulations restricting how long child actors are lawfully allowed to work in any time period were not created with the intention of limiting methods of competition between car companies.[85] The logical conclusion of this argument is that in defining what counts as 'unlawful means' for the purposes of the tort courts should consider whether the means involved should be a forbidden method in advancing competition or protest.

The choice between the possible definitions of 'unlawful means' may be of particular importance in the on-line context because implementation of the Directive on e-commerce is likely to lead to several forms of behaviour becoming 'unlawful means' in the sense of 'acts one is not at liberty to commit', but for reasons other than a desire to restrict methods of competition and protest. For instance, implementation of Article 5 will lead to it being obligatory for service providers to, for instance, make available their geographic addresses, and to indicate unambiguously whether prices are inclusive of delivery. But it is far from clear that breach of such an obligation by a website that is specifically aimed at another's business should be sufficient to trigger the tort.

Whilst an over-broad definition of 'unlawful means' may lead to over protection of e-businesses against competition and protest, it seems probable that a greater problem will be the under-protection likely to follow from English law's insistence that the means used are independently unlawful. If English law instead relied on a concept of 'unacceptable means' or 'means contrary to good business ethics' it would

---

82 Defining 'unlawful means' as 'what you have no legal right to do' is commended by P. Sales and D. Stilitz, 'Intentional infliction of Harm by Unlawful Means', LQR 115 (1999) 411, at 414. It must be assumed that the word 'right' is used loosely in this formulation. Consequently, Lord Denning MR's phrase, 'by an act which he is not at liberty to commit' may be preferable: *Torquay Hotel Co* v. *Cousins* [1969] 2 Ch. 106.

83 Not every author agrees that 'acts he is not at liberty to commit' is a *clear* definition. H. Carty, *An Analysis of the Economic Torts* (Oxford University Press, Oxford, 2001), p.125-6 argues that the definition is imprecise, and (p. 127-8, 274) that the definition should be 'wrongs capable of being civilly actionable with a right to damages'.

84 This is the view supported by N. McBride and R. Bagshaw, *Tort Law* (Longman, Harlow, 2001), p. 352.

85 A parallel example could be produced with the child actor being used in the production of an advertisement directed at C by a protest group.

have a better chance of dealing appropriately with new 'means' of interference with trade that have only emerged in the on-line environment:[86] For instance, setting up web businesses or protest sites with addresses based on common mis-spellings of a rival's name, common (but unregistered) nicknames associated with a rival, and the rival's name incorporated into a longer word.[87]

6 Provisional conclusions

It is a trite observation that tort law seeks to balance the need to protect certain interests against freedom of action. Consequently, in so far as the on-line world creates new protectable interests, new ways of exposing protectable interests to the risk of harm, and new varieties of behaviour which may harm protectable interests, it creates new challenges for tort law.

This contribution, up to this point, has not addressed the question whether the on-line world has created new protectable interests. The question of how to classify 'damage to data' is on the borderline of this category, but data can exist outside an on-line world. No doubt, however, the on-line world will make this issue more pressing, with data being damaged by the cutting of cables, accidental or deliberate transmission of viruses, and the activities of 'script-kiddies'. Beyond this, there is some scope for imagining the eventual recognition of new forms of harm. For instance, if human beings choose to project themselves as characters that exist solely in a cyberworld there may be issues relating to assaults on those projected-characters quite apart from any indirect distress to the human beings behind them. Such a suggestion is currently towards the edge of science fiction, but can we not imagine Walt Disney wanting to sue a defendant who 'burnt' an effigy of Mickey Mouse on line? (quite apart from any copyright issues or any distress to Disney executives). Similarly, online games players are already paying significant sums for property that exists solely in a virtual world.[88] No doubt legal disputes will soon arise.[89]

Most of the discussion in this contribution concerns new forms of human interaction made possible by the on-line world, and the new ways in which these interac-

---

86 The issues relating to use of hyperlinks are an excellent example, and are discussed elsewhere in this collection.

87 E.g. bagshaw.co.uk might face competition or protest from baghsaw.co.uk and bagshawsafool.co.uk. Although the Uniform Domain Name Dispute Resolution Policy contains provisions and procedures which may allow the reallocation of domain names it expressly does not allow for the award of compensation. Consequently, parties may still want to resort to unfair competition torts. The on-line collection of 'cease and desist' letters maintained by the Chilling Effects Clearinghouse (a joint project of several leading US Law Schools) provides evidence of the frequency with which 'unfair competition' is alleged against parody and protest sites <www.chillingeffects.org/notice.cgi>.

88 One of the most popular multiplayer virtual world games can be experienced at Ultima On line <www.uo.com/visitor/>. At the time of writing (October 2002) a search of 'uo' items for sale on www.ebay.com yielded 1761 items, many of which only existed online, such as an 'ethereal unicorn', some 'blessed black sandals' and a 'log cabin near Skara Brae Moongate'.

89 E.g. is it possible to take a bailment of on-line property? If so, can there be liability for negligent custodianship?

tions may expose traditionally protected interests to the risk of harm. Nothing written above suggests that tort law will be incapable of dealing with these new situations. But perhaps there is enough to suggest that the adaptation of traditional tort doctrine to cyberworld will not be as straightforward as 'downloading' doctrine from off-line contexts.[90]

90 Anyone still not convinced by this may want to consider areas of law other than torts. For instance, how the principles of trademarks law have been altered by domain names and search engines.

The moment of effectiveness of e-mail notices

Henk Snijders

1 LEGAL CONTEXT

The Netherlands Civil Code (BW) provides for a simple answer to the question of the formation of contracts. Article 6:217 BW states that 'a contract is formed by an offer and its acceptance'. Both the offer and the acceptance are juridical acts in the sense of title 2 of book 3 BW. Article 3:37, §3 BW states on juridical acts:

> A declaration made to a specifically determined person, in order to be effective, must have reached that person. Nevertheless, even a declaration which has not reached the person to whom it was made, or has not reached him in time, does have effect if this situation results from his own act, from the act of persons for whom he is responsible, or from other circumstances which are personal to him and justify that he suffer the consequences.

The question arising in the context of e-commerce contracts is what to think of an e-mail declaration intended for a certain juridical act such as the offer or acceptance of an e-commerce contract in case the addressee does not receive the declaration and/or does not take cognisance of it, for instance because

(a) he does not open his e-mailbox or he accidentally wipes the e-mail notice to be taken into consideration, or
(b) the service provider of the intended addressee wipes the e-mail notice, or ceases its service so that the e-mail notice cannot be opened by the addressee, or
(c) the addressee becomes the victim of a computer crash, a hacker or a computer virus, due to which the e-mail notice does not arrive.

The meaning of the second sentence of art. 3:37, §3 BW, cannot be made clear as long as the meaning of the first sentence remains unclear. In other words, we can observe that as far as the conditions for 'reaching' in the meaning of the first sentence of art. 3.37, §3 BW are stricter, the need for exceptions such as mentioned in the second sentence of art. 3:37, §3 BW will become stronger. That is why we must pay attention to the meaning of the first sentence in the first place. This analysis will be made within the context of supranational and international law.

2 THE MEANING OF 'REACHING'

It is remarkable that there is still discussion on the meaning of the verb 'reaching' in art. 3.37, §3, first sentence BW. This discussion focuses on the question whether the receipt of the declaration by the addressee is sufficient as such (the 'receipt theory'), or whether the addressee must have taken cognisance of the notice as well (the 'cog-

H. Snijders, S. Weatherill (eds.), *E-commerce Law*, 79-88

nisance theory'). The official explanation of this provision by the main author of the Netherlands Civil Code, the former Leiden professor of civil law E.M. Meijers[1], and the official explanation of the government for this provision point to the interpretation of the word 'reaching' as 'being received' only.

Before dealing with other authorities, it seems appropriate to make some remarks with respect to the content of arguments for and against the 'receipt theory' and the cognisance theory for the formation of juridical acts.

Unconditional application of the cognisance theory provides the addressee of a declaration with an opportunity to prevent it from reaching him. Doing so he would be able to prevent the formation of the unilateral juridical act, which was specifically addressed to him.[2] This argument could be rendered harmless, indeed, by adding conditions for the application of the cognisance theory. Exceptions to the second sentence of art. 3:37, §3 could be used as a countermeasure.

Another argument against the cognisance theory is, again, given by Meijers in the first-mentioned authority: it is not practical to demand that the sender prove not only that his declaration has been received by the addressee but read by the latter as well. Nor would such a requirement be reasonable. It is possible, of course, to require this through interpretation of the first sentence of art. 3:37, §3 BW on the one hand and to accept a general exception by way of application of the second sentence of art 3:37, §3 BW on the other hand. Doing so, however, the interpreter shows that this alternative to the interpretation of the first sentence actually is unacceptable .

Of course, there are also arguments against the receipt theory. One objection we can find in the literature is that there is always some time between receiving and reading a declaration.[3] The question is, however, whether or not the moment of reading is relevant. A offers his car to B on December 1st, adding that acceptance of the offer has to be realised at the latest on December 10th. B accepts the offer by letter of December 8th. The letter falls into A's letterbox on December 10th; A reads the letter on December 11th. It can be stated that the latter fact is irrelevant. A is authorised to decide when he wants to open his letters, but he is not authorised to decide on the exact moment of the formation of a unilateral juridical act by another person: that other person – B – has done everything necessary for the letter to reach A. B's acting including the actions needed from other persons (such as the postman) has been completed. B can do nothing anymore to prevent the juridical act from coming about.

Another argument against the receipt theory is that this theory would be too rigid and would be unreasonable in its outcomes. Supposing, for instance, that the letter is put in the letterbox after office hours, it would be unreasonable to expect this letter to be read before the next morning. However, it must be considered irrelevant what the

1 Parlementaire Geschiedenis book 3, p. 182: first, second and third full paragraph resp. book 6, p. 890.

2 See e.g. Mr. C. Asser's handleiding tot de beoefening van het Nederlands burgerlijk recht, bewerkt door A.S. Hartkamp (Deventer: Tjeenk Willink 2001), nos. 152-153, and A.R. Bloembergen, C.C. van Dam, Jac. Hijma & W.L. Valk, *Rechtshandeling en overeenkomst* (Kluwer: Deventer 2001), no. 29.

3 See e.g. Asser/Hartkamp 2001 (see note 2).

sender may expect concerning the time of reading. Supposing that B's letter in the case just mentioned had fallen into the letterbox after office hours, then B would have done, again, everything necessary to reach A. He would have completed all his actions, including actions of other persons necessary for the receipt by A, and he would have had no possibility of preventing the formation of the intended juridical act. Now supposing that a person can subscribe for participation in a company, in conformity with the announcement of his bank on December 10th at the latest, is the banking company then justified in stating that the subscriber is really too late if he puts his subscription form in the letterbox after office hours on December 10th? And what about the case in which the letter has been sent by post and -for instance, because of weather conditions- the postman puts the letter in the letterbox after office hours on December 10th? Does it really matter at what time the subscription form is taken from the letterbox and even: does it matter when the form is read? Another question is whether or not the sender is able to prove that he did indeed put the subscription form in the letterbox or that another person -such as the postman- did it for him. Similar problems could arise when he delivered the form just before closing time and the letterbox was opened only the next day. No existing theory on the meaning of 'reaching' fully resolves the problem of proof.

The Netherlands Supreme Court is disposed towards the receipt theory. This applies both to the moment of effectiveness of procedural documents such as requests and to the moment of effectiveness of other juridical acts.[4]

Supranational and international sources refer to the acceptance of the receipt theory as well.

Article 24 of the United Nations on the Contracts for the International Sale of Goods states:

> For the purposes of this Part of the Convention (Part II, Formation of the Contract: HJS), an offer, declaration of acceptance or any other indication or intention 'reaches' the addressee when it is made orally to him or delivered by any other means to him personally, to his place of business or mailing address or, if he does not have a place of business or mailing address, to his habitual residence.

This provision clearly supports the receipt theory for written declarations (for other declarations it is supposed that receipt and cognisance are realised at the same moment, but this is not so evident in our time of answering machines and voice mail techniques.[5]) Article 24 follows articles 15 and 18 of the Treaty, which consider it de-

---

4 See e.g. HR June 10 1994, *NJ* 1995, 284; HR Feb. 16 1996, NJ 1997, 95; HR Mar. 20 1998, NJ 1998, 548; HR Sept. 8 1995; NJ 1996, 567. See for discussions on the interpretation of the Supreme Court on this question H.J. Snijders, 'Het bereiken van een geadresseerde (per e-mail) I en II, slot, WPNR 2001, p. 6444-6445. Other questions concerning the moment of effectiveness of (e-mail) notices are dealt with in greater detail in that article, too.

5 There are still authors who suppose the same as article 24 of the just-mentioned treaty does: see e.g. Hein Kötz & Axel Flessner, *European Contract Law* (Oxford 1997), p. 20-21 ('An offer made orally or by telephone reaches the addressee as soon as he hears it').

cisive for both offer and acceptance at which moment these notices reach the addressee.

The same applies to the UNIDROIT Principles for International Commercial Contracts, which state in Article 1.9:

> (2) A notice is effective when it reaches a person to whom it is given.
> (3) For the purpose of Paragraph (2) a notice 'reaches' a person when given to that person orally or delivered at that person's place of business or mailing address.

Both for the offer (art. 2.3, §1) and for the acceptance (art. 2.6, §2) it is expressly stated that as far as it concerns the formation the question is when the notice reaches the addressee in the sense of art. 1.9, §2-3. In the official explanation of art.1.9 it can be read that for non-oral notices it is sufficient:

> that it be handed over to an employee of the addressee authorized to accept it, or that it be placed in the addressee's fax, telex or computer.

One may wonder if the authors of the explanation have realised that many e-mail notices reach the addressee through his mailbox and, consequently, that the question is whether receipt in the e-mailbox of the addressee is decisive or the actual receipt in his computer. We will deal with this question further on.

The European Principles of Contract Law (EPCL) of the Lando commission[6] include in art. 2:205:

> If an acceptance has been dispatched by the offeree the contract is concluded when the acceptance reaches the offeror.

The official explanation[7] makes it clear that the verb 'reaching' is understood to mean 'receiving'. The theory that it matters 'when the acceptance reaches the offeror' is here called the 'receipt rule'.

Finally the European Directive on e-commerce[8] can be mentioned, which states in article 11 under the subtitle 'Placing of the order':

> The order and the acknowledgement of receipt are deemed to be received when the parties to whom they are addressed are able to access them.

Although the E-commerce Directive does not fix the moment of formation of an online contract very clearly, we can consider this phrase as a support for the receipt theory: not the cognisance but the receipt is mentioned as a criterion in this provision under the subtitle 'placing of the order'.

It would take us too far to deal with the multitude of domestic law systems on this question. Short characteristics will do: undoubtedly, the receipt theory is number

---

6 O. Lando & H. Beale (ed.), *European Principles of Contract Law. Parts I and II* (Kluwer Law International: The Hague/London/Boston, 2000), p. 137 ff.

7 Lando & Beale 2000, footnote 2 p. 173 (see note 6).

8 June 8 2000 PbEG L 178.

one; the so-called sending theory, which implies that the moment of sending is decisive, can be considered number two.[9]

Considering supranational, international and foreign law sources and supposing that a new European Civil Code will be established (in the distant future), it seems quite probable that this Code would accept the receipt theory and not the cognisance theory. Countries which accept the sending theory in their domestic law system would just accept the receipt theory, whereas the step to the cognisance theory could be a 'bridge too far'.

3 CORRECTIONS OF AND EXCEPTIONS TO THE RECEIPT RULE

It has to be added that most supporters of the receipt theory still tend to apply a correction in favour of the cognisance theory in certain types of cases. This need for correction becomes clear when we realise the consequences of unconditional application of the receipt theory. From that point of view the first sentence of art. 3:37, §3BW, could be elaborated for instance in this sense that the declaration is supposed to reach the addressee at the moment that he receives it, unless he has not taken cognisance of it at this moment, and no normal person could have taken cognisance of the notice at that moment under the given non-personal circumstances.This elaborating correction of article 3:37, §3, first sentence BW, could still be refined further. The correction is only reasonable if the reading is essential for the addressee in the given circumstances (and supposing that the addressee wants to raise the objection of the impossibility of reading to the sender). In other words, it can be held that the addressee must have a reasonable interest in invoking the impossibility of reading to the sender.

Another reason to correct for the addressee's inability to read the notice, could be personal handicaps or other personal circumstances, in case the sender misused those circumstances. Anyone who, knowingly, sends a notice by post to a single blind person should accept the objection that his declaration did not reach this person: despite the receipt of the declaration it cannot be considered to be a juridical act. Abuse of the receipt theory must be prevented.

The same applies for other circumstances which ought to be at the risk of the addressee, such as the circumstances mentioned in the second sentence of art. 3:37, §3 BW. Again, it must be possible to prevent abuse of rights. In his explanation on art. 3:37 BW (l.c.) Meijers says that if the sender was familiar with the particular personal circumstances of the addressee, it is rather a mistake of the sender to ignore these circumstances, which occasioned the non-receipt of the declaration.

Considering the need for corrections of and exceptions to the receipt theory, we can conclude that they are all inspired by the idea of reasonableness. It concerns circum-

9 See e.g. the official explanation of art. 2: 205 EPCL (see note 6), Kötz & Flessner 1997, p. 20-21 (see note 5), D.A. Levy, Uniform Commercial Code Journal 1997 (vol. 30, No. 3), p. 273-274 (the Uniform Commercial Code accepts the receipt theory as well), resp. Heather Row International Business Lawyer 1998, p. 165 ff.

stances in which invoking the receipt theory, and a fortiori invoking the second sentence of art. 3:37, § 3 BW, in spite of the inability to read the declaration, is absolutely unreasonable. In these cases the argument of the addressee can be supported in the Netherlands by art. 6:2, §2 BW and art. 6:248, §2 BW, stating respectively:

1. A creditor and debtor must, as between themselves, act in accordance with the requirements of reasonableness and equity.
2. A rule binding upon them by virtue of law, usage or a juridical act does not apply to the extent that, in the given circumstances, this would be unacceptable according to criteria of reasonableness and equity.'

and

1. A contract has not only the juridical effects agreed to by the parties, but also those which, according to the nature of the contract, result from the law, usage or the requirements of reasonableness and equity.
2. A rule binding upon the parties as a result of the contract does not apply to the extent that, in the given circumstances, this would be unacceptable according to criteria of reasonableness and equity.

Support for this opinion can also be found in art. 7, §1 of the United Nations Convention on the State of Goods, stating that the interpretation of the Treaty requires taking into account 'the observation of good faith in international trade'. For the sender the reasonableness corrective can be a danger. In order to be sure that the intended juridical act comes about, he has to choose a way of communication that assures a very quick cognisance after receipt of this declaration **and** proof of that. And indeed, that is what often happens in e-commerce practice. Another way of managing this problem is using several ways of communication at the same time. And that is, indeed, what happens in practice as well (it is comparable to the law firm's attitude of sending important messages to counterparts both by post and by fax).

4 So far for declarations in general, but what about e-mail declarations?

Of course, it is possible that the formation of the juridical act by e-mail is prevented because it does not fulfil the applicable form conditions. However, according to the European Directive on E-commerce many form conditions must be eliminated. See in particular article 9 of the Directive, which, in general, imposes on Member States the obligation to accept electronic contracts and forbids them to maintain rules which invalidate contracts for the mere reason of being established through electronic means.

Thus, the starting point can be that there are no form conditions which prevent the formation of a juridical act by e-mail and from this point we can answer the question at which moment an e-mail notice becomes effective.

The first partial answer to the question of the moment of effectiveness of an email-notice is self-evident following the foregoing considerations: in general, not the moment of reading by the addressee but the moment of its receipt is decisive for the formation of the juridical act, which possibly is intended to be laid down in the e-mail notice; even the receipt is not necessary in the circumstances mentioned in the second sentence of art. 3:37, §3 BW. The reasonableness corrective mentioned above can be applied here as well.

Supposing, however, that e-mail does not reach the addressee directly, but through his e-mailbox: which moment should be considered as the moment of receipt of the e-mail notice? Is it the moment of putting it in his e-mailbox or the moment he collects the e-mail notice from his e-mailbox? In other words: do we accept the 'mailbox -receipt theory' or the 'computer-receipt theory'? Anyone who considers the e-mailbox as a normal post office box will consider the moment of receipt in the e-mailbox as decisive, and the question is whether or not that equal treatment is justified.

Just like some other authors[10] and, meanwhile, our government,[11] this author finds for the conclusion that the e-mailbox has, indeed, to be dealt with as a normal post office box. The sender would have done everything necessary to reach the addressee including the actions needed from other persons (such as the service provider). He can do nothing anymore to prevent the juridical act from coming about. It is true that the service provider could close the e-mailbox, or empty it after receipt but before the collection of the e-mail by the addressee. However, this kind of attitude seems to be so atypical, that it is not justified here to state the argument the sender has not done everything to reach the addressee. In general, service providers do not make a habit of ending their services from one day to the next. Mala fide clearing operations of service providers seem, in general, like science fiction as well. What is more, even traditional national post companies are able to block or empty the post office box of an addressee after receipt and before collection , yet this possibility is not supposed to hinder the acceptance of receipt at the moment the notice is put into the post office box.

Receipt in an e-mail box can be even more secure than receipt in a traditional physical post office box. Getting the addressee's service provider's 'confirmation of delivery' the sender can be sure (like the sender of the fax, who receives a confirmation report with 'status OK') that the addressee has received the notice, that is, in his e-mail box at least.

From this point of view it is understandable that in the Draft Uniform Rules for Electronic Trade Settlement (URETS) of the International Chamber of Commerce for offer and acceptance the following model clause has been proposed, that such a ju-

---

10 R.E. van Esch, Electronic Data Interchange (EDI) en het vermogensrecht (W.E.J. Tjeenk Willink: Deventer 1999) (diss. KUN), p. 98 ff., supported by C. Stuurman in the *Netherlands Civil Law Review* (NTBR) 2000, p. 28; Rolph H. Weber, *Informatikrecht im europäischen Umfelt*, Schulthess Polygraphischer Verlag: Zürich 1997, p. 247, Van der Wiel l.c., B.J. Broekema-Engelen and J.W. Broekema, 'De werking van een verklaring: ontvangsttheorie ook van toepassing bij moderne communicatiemiddelen', Bb 1999, p. 221-222. See also F.A.M. van der Klaauw-Koops in: R.E. van Esch & C. Prins, *Recht en EDI: juridische aspecten van elektronisch berichtenverkeer* (Deventer: Kluwer 2001), p. 43.

11 In the official explanation of the Bill on the implementation of the European Directive on E-commerce, *Kamerstukken II* 2001/2002, 28 197, nr. 3, p. 59.

ridical act 'becomes effective when it enters the information system of the recipient in a form capable of being processed by that system'.[12]

The above-mentioned correctives -the reasonableness corrective in the narrow sense and the corrective on the basis of abuse of rights- can be applied as well. There is no reason, for instance, for another approach to e-mail notices only because the addressee does not often open his e-mailbox.[13] We can refer for this point of view to the existing opinions on ways of communication, such as using post office box and letterbox.

Another exception, which has been pleaded for, concerns the notice equipped with an encryption by the sender, so that the addressee cannot open it.[14] It seems that such a notice cannot be considered a juridical act for other reasons, because art. 3:33 BW requires the intention to produce juridical effects which has to manifest itself by declaration and in this case the manifestation requirement is not fulfilled.

In favour of the mailbox-receipt theory also it has been argued that the theory meets the need for legal security.[15] The moment of receipt in the addressee's computer can be observed more or less safely on the basis of a 'confirmation of reading'. The mailbox-receipt theory will, however, just like the computer-receipt theory, require reasonableness correctives, so the legal security will remain problematic in both theories.

Finally it may be mentioned that the sender and the addressee are, of course, allowed to agree that the cognisance instead of the receipt, or the receipt in the computer instead of the receipt in the e-mailbox, is decisive.[16] The contracting parties can agree as well that only after confirmation of the receipt of an e-mail notice does the juridical act intended in that notice come about (the original system for exclusively electronic and similar contracts of the draft Directive on e-commerce, which has been left finally). Another possibility: the parties agree that the e-mail notice must be considered invalid if its receipt is not confirmed within a certain period (as in art. 5.4 of the European EDI-model contract and in conformity with the suggestion of art. 14 UNCITRAL Model Law on Electronic Commerce (1996)). We have still to realise that this kind of agreement solves one problem, but creates a new one: even for that confirmation of receipt the question arises at which moment the notice reaches the addressee. The same applies to art. 6:227, par. 2 BW, as proposed in our Bill on the implementation of the European Directive on E-commerce, stating that as long as the receipt of an acceptance has not been confirmed, the other party is allowed to undo the agreement and that non-timely confirmation of the receipt of an offer is deemed to be considered as a rejection of the offer.

---

12 There is, however, some criticism on this model clause. See R.E. van Esch, 'Concept Uniform Rules for Electronic Trade and Settlement (URETS) van de Internationale Kamer van Koophandel, *Contracteren* 2000, p. 54, stating that the point of view that every electronic declaration can be dealt with without any human intervention applies to EDI-notices, but not to e-mail notices in general.

13 Otherwise Van Esch 1999, p. 101 (see note 10).

14 See Van Esch 1999 (see note 10).

15 Van Esch 1999, p. 99-100 (see note 10).

16 See also -inter alia- Peter K. Neuenschwander in Informatikrecht p. 179 ff. and Van Esch 1999, p.103 and 107 (see note 10), who give examples of model interchange agreements.

Following the foregoing considerations of §3 and §4 again, the question whether an electronic declaration has reached the addressee seems in general irrespective of his personal context. Even the reasonableness corrective in the narrow sense does not come into action for the only reason that the addressee has no possibility of taking cognisance of a declaration, but, in general, only if any normal person were unable to take cognisance of an electronic declaration under the circumstances of the case, excluding personal circumstances of the addressee. This personal context is only important in the sense that abuse of it can be sanctioned by upholding the effectiveness of the e-mail notice, as explained before.

5 Back to the cases of paragraph 1

Now the time has come to deal with the cases of the first paragraph of this contribution in greater detail, taking into account both components of art. 3:37, §3 BW.

First of all, case (a): the addressee does not open his e-mailbox or he accidentally wipes the e-mail notice to be taken into consideration.

On the basis of the receipt theory and in particular the mailbox-receipt theory, these circumstances do not matter: the declaration has reached the addressee meanwhile. An exception on the basis of the reasonableness corrective in the narrow sense does not work here either.[17] Abuse of rights will not be often at stake in this case. On the basis of the computer-receipt theory, the declaration has not reached the addressee. It can be argued that this is a consequence of his own acting in the sense of art.3: 37, § 3, second sentence BW and, thus, that the intended juridical act can still become effective. What has been argued on the basis of the computer-receipt theory can also be argued on the basis of the cognisance theory.

Then case (b): the service provider of the intended addressee wipes the e-mail notice, or ceases its service so that the addressee cannot open the e-mail notice.

On the basis of the mailbox receipt theory, the circumstances do not matter, in principle: the declaration has reached the addressee meanwhile. The reasonableness corrective in the narrow sense does not work here either, because there are personal circumstances of the addressee at stake. However, an exception can be made, then, for abuse of rights. On the basis of the computer-receipt theory the declaration has not reached the addressee. This is the consequence of the action of a person for which the addressee is responsible in the sense of art. 3:37, § 3, second sentence BW so that the intended juridical act can still become effective except abuse of rights.[18] What has been argued on the basis of the computer-receipt theory can be argued on the basis of the cognisance theory as well.

17 See also Meijers explanation, PG book 3, p. 182 and book 6, p. 98.

18 Meijers in his explanation mentions the example of the letter which has been given to a subordinate of the addressee without the subordinate passing the message to the addressee.

Finally case (c): the addressee becomes the victim of a computer crash, a hacker or a computer virus, as a result of which the e-mail notice does not arrive.

On the basis of the mailbox-receipt-theory, these circumstances do not matter in principle: the declaration has reached the addressee meanwhile. One could argue that the reasonableness corrective in the narrow sense might work here, because the addressee could reasonably not take cognisance of the declaration. However, it will concern the addressee's personal circumstances, which have to be at his risk, except, again, for the abuse of rights. On the basis of the computer-receipt theory, the declaration has possibly reached the addressee. If so, the same applies as just argued on the basis of the mailbox-receipt theory. If not, it can be argued that the declaration's not reaching the addressee will often be caused by 'other circumstances which are personal to him and justify that he suffer the consequences' as provided for in art. 3:37, § 3, second sentence BW, so that the intended juridical act can still become effective.[19] This applies, except, again, in case of abuse of rights. What has been argued on the basis of the computer-receipt theory, applies on the basis of the cognisance theory as well.

This analysis shows that the receipt theory -both the mailbox-receipt theory and the computer-receipt theory- and the cognisance theory can lead to the same result, supposing the applicability of the reasonableness corrective in the narrow sense and the corrective on the basis of abuse of rights. In the author's opinion it would be a good thing to end discussions on the question whether the receipt theory or the cognisance theory is the better one. Supranational, international, foreign and domestic authorities mainly point to the receipt theory as the winning concept. Let us greet this theory, and in particular the mailbox receipt theory, with open arms in future and concentrate on questions that are really important, such as the question under which circumstances we have to leave it at the addressee's risk that the message does not reach him by e-mail. The analysis also shows a couple of ideas for the solution of cases of the last-mentioned signature.

---

19 Meijers in his explanation mentions the example that the addressee has had a traffic accident and has been hospitalised. This applies, except, again, for the sender's abuse of rights.

Caveat emptor in digital times

Hans Nieuwenhuis

1 DID YOU EVER SEE TWO COMPUTERS MAKE A FAIR AND DELIBERATE EXCHANGE?

'Nobody ever saw a dog make a fair and deliberate exchange of one bone for another with another dog.' Making contracts is 'common to all men, and to be found in no other race of animals'. Thus, Adam Smith in his *Wealth of Nations.*[1]

No race of animals other than the homo sapiens? How about computers?

Did you ever see two computers make a fair and deliberate exchange?

This seems to be a piece of cake. A valid contract can be concluded by two 'electronic agents', i.e. 'computer programs used independently to respond to electronic messages without intervention by an individual at the time of the response.'

The electronic agent of a bookseller, finding out that there are only three copies of 'An Introduction to Comparative Law' in stock, spontaneously buys fifty copies from the electronic agent of the Oxford University Press. Electronic contracts can, of course, also be concluded between a human being and an electronic agent. This will be the case if I add *Bleak House* to my 'on line shopping cart' provided by Amazon.com.

Everyone agrees that electronic agents are not real agents as understood by the law of agency. You can only act as an agent, representing your principal at the conclusion of a contract, if you are a person, be it a natural person or a legal person.

The responses made by the electronic agent show a close resemblance to the reactions of a Pavlov dog. This may be a very intelligent dog, performing very complicated tasks, but its choices are not its own. His master's voice is all there is to obey. Its behaviour is completely determined by the way in which it is programmed. Likewise, an electronic agent may be able, far better than I am, to find out whether Alitalia offers lower prices for flying from Amsterdam to Rome than KLM, but only I am able to decide whether it is advisable for me to fly to Rome, rather than buy a new dishwasher.

Some key concepts of Contract Law seem to be linked exclusively to human nature: the principle of good faith and fair dealing, for instance. This principle is one of the cornerstones of the new Principles of European Contract Law:

> Each party must act in accordance with good faith and fair dealing. (Article 1:201).

It may not be absurd to speak of a dog being faithful and fair, but as regards an electronic agent, the requirements of good faith and fair dealing can only apply to the person employing this agent and to the ways in which he has programmed it.

---

1 Adam Smith, *An inquiry into the nature and causes of the wealth of nations*, ch. 2.

H. Snijders, S. Weatherill (eds.), *E-commerce Law*, 89-92

How is one to instruct an electronic agent in order to have it act in accordance with good faith and fair dealing? Take for instance the concept of fundamental mistake in the Principles of European Contract Law:

> A party may avoid a contract for mistake (...) if the other party knew or ought to have known of the mistake and it was contrary to good faith and fair dealing to leave the mistaken party in error. (Article 4:103).

The principle of good faith and fair dealing is especially tailored for face-to-face situations. If I have reasons to believe that the person wanting to buy my farm is mistaken about the number of pigs he is allowed to breed there, I may have to inform him, even if he did not question me on this point. The homely wisdom, 'Ask me no questions and I will tell you no lies' is not a safe guideline in Contract Law.

What applies 'Off line', should also apply 'On line'. This is a recurrent theme in the debate on the law relating to e-commerce. Legal principles and norms governing the 'Off-line' situation, where both parties are physically present when negotiating a contract, should also apply if the contract is concluded 'On line'.

Amazon.com ought to know that several people are seriously mistaken about their ability to understand and appreciate 'Finnegans Wake' by James Joyce. Should Amazon give them the opportunity to test their ability by confronting them with the first sentence?:

> riverrun, past Eve and Adam's, from swerve of shore to bend of bay, brings us by a commodius vicus of recirculation back to Howth Castle and Environs?[2]

Irrespective of whether the contract is to be concluded 'Off line', or 'On line', Contract Law should try to strike a fair balance between two opposing principles: on the one hand, the principle of *Caveat Emptor*, let the buyer beware, and on the other hand, the altruistic principle that you have to inform the other party if you know him to be mistaken. *Caveat Emptor* tells a person wanting to buy a second-hand car to have this car properly inspected **before** concluding the contract. But in some cases, for instance, if the seller is a professional seller of second-hand cars, Dutch Contract Law requires that the seller inform the buyer that this car has been involved in a serious crash and that the damage has been repaired rather inadequately.

2 *CAVEAT EMPTOR* 'ON LINE'

What's the meaning of *Caveat Emptor* 'On line'? Browsing the web, you discover an attractive KitchenAid Ultra Power Food Processor priced at € 199. But you are not sure whether you can handle this high-tech device. At this point a Directive of the European Community comes to your aid:

---

2 In fact, <www.amazon.com> offers the opportunity to inspect, not only the front and back covers and table of contents, but also some eight sample pages of *Finnegans Wake*.

> For any distance contract the consumer shall have a period of at least seven working days in which to withdraw from the contract without penalty and without giving any reason. The only charge that may be made to the consumer because of the exercise of his right of withdrawal is the direct cost of returning the goods. The period for exercise of this right shall begin: in case of goods, from the day of receipt by the consumer (...)' (Directive 97/7/EC, Article 6).

The consumer has ample opportunity to heed the warning: *Caveat Emptor*. Seven days and seven nights he can test the Ultra Power Food Processor and in the end decide: I prefer my old set of kitchen knives. He can then withdraw from the contract without giving any reason.

Can we still call this European consumer distance contract a contract? What is left of the binding nature of a contract if one of the parties is allowed to withdraw from it at will? Medieval civil lawyers, commenting upon Digest 19,1,13,29, would call this arrangement a negotium claudicans, a limping contract:

> si quis a pupillo sine tutoris auctoritate emerit, ex uno latere constat contractus.
> If a man buys from a *pupillus* without his tutor's authorisation, a contract arises on one side only. (translation A.Watson).

There is, however, an important difference between the merchant in Roman times and the modern dot.com firm. The Roman merchant could easily avoid concluding contracts with pupilli (boys younger than fourteen). Modern e-commerce firms, on the other hand, can hardly be expected to avoid doing business with adult consumers. Is this unconditional right to withdraw from the contract fair to the seller? One could object that it is not so much a question of fairness, but of Law and Economics.

Economics first: any higher level of consumer protection is in the end paid by the consumers. Every 'On-line' seller will estimate the percentage of goods that will be returned by consumers deciding to withdraw from the contract. In those cases he not only loses the costs of shipping these goods to the consumer, even if it were agreed that the consumer should pay these costs, but he will also be unable to resell these returned goods – food processors for instance – as new and unused. In calculating the price of his products, he will have to take these losses into account.

Now, turning to the law: how is one to 'withdraw' from the contract?

According to the American singer Paul Simon there are fifty ways to leave your lover, some quite subtle: hop on the bus, Gus; make a new plan, Stan.

In Dutch Law there are two distinct, far less subtle, ways to leave a contract. The first uses retroactive force: annul the contract. The contract is considered to have been null and void from the start (ex tunc). If ownership has been transferred, it automatically returns to the seller. The second way in which to leave a contract is to terminate the contract ex nunc. The contract stays valid for the period preceding its termination. If ownership has been transferred, it must be transferred back.

Implementing the Directive, the Netherlands have opted for the second technique. On receiving the goods bought 'On line' ownership is transferred to the buyer. If after seven days he decides to terminate the contract, the buyer must transfer the ownership back to the seller.

The fact that during the trial period of seven days the buyer, and not the seller, is the owner of the goods causes problems in case of bankruptcy of the buyer. A bankruptcy will block the transfer of ownership back to the seller.

Can the seller forestall these complications by simply stipulating a retention of ownership (reservation of title)?

Under Dutch law a retention of ownership by the seller is only valid if it is meant to ensure payment by the buyer (Article 3: 92 Civil Code). Buying On line' the consumer will normally have paid before receiving the goods. A retention of ownership is therefore ineffective.

What's the most effective remedy for chronic headaches?

The guillotine, without any doubt. Chop off your head and your headache will most certainly disappear. But the most effective remedy is not always the best. It might contain some overkill. New developments in law often contain a considerable amount of overkill. Take the development of a non-possessory security for movables in German and Dutch law. It started as a fiduciary transfer of ownership in combination with a delivery per constitutum possessorium. Thus, the goods could remain with the transferor. Next it became urgent to trim this fiduciary ownership to reasonable proportions in order to protect the rights of third parties. The *Hoge Raad* did this in an impressive series of decisions. This opened the way for a more balanced device for non-possessory security on movables in our new Civil Code: a right of pledge which can be established without bringing the goods under the control of the creditor (Article 3: 237 Civil Code).

A similar development in the way in which we construe the right to withdraw from the 'On-line' contract is very likely. Again, the law concerning 'On-line' contracts should follow the example offered by the 'Off-line' world as closely as possible.

A voice from the real world: A wants to sell his caravanette for € 10,000 to B (**caravanette,** a motor vehicle with a caravan-like rear compartment for eating, sleeping etc.; Concise Oxford Dictionary). The price is no problem for B, but he would like to test whether he can handle the car. In order to win him over A allows B to try the caravanette during the weekend. After the weekend B tells A that he thorougly disliked the eating and sleeping facilities. B hands the caravanette back to A.

No one would deem it necessary to construe these facts in such a way as to imply that on Friday A sold the caravanette to B and transferred the ownership thereof, and that on Monday B terminated the contract and transferred the ownership back to A. Far more realistic is the view that on Friday A made an offer to B, and on Monday B declined this offer.

Likewise, we should construe the response of the electronic agent of an 'On-line' seller and the subsequent shipping of the goods as an offer which is irrevocable during a period of seven days after receipt. In this way a serious problem will disappear. Both in 'Off-line' and in 'On-line' commerce we should keep two activities clearly apart: one, finding out whether a proposed contract suits us, and two, concluding the contract. The *Caveat Emptor* principle belongs to the former and should not cross borders with the latter. Once the contract has been concluded another principle should reign: *Pacta sunt servanda.*

The promise and peril of spontaneous order: the role of government in shaping e-commerce

Josh Holmes and Bronwen Morgan

1 Introduction

When considering how to regulate Internet-assisted markets, discussion typically focuses upon how, if at all, this new technological medium differs from more conventional methods of transacting. Our aim here is to examine the implications and limits of one particular perspective upon the distinctiveness of the Internet. The approach we have in mind emphasises the Internet's potential to operate as a self-constituting or spontaneous order in which individual human endeavours combine, without the agency of any central system of coordination, to produce a workable and mutually advantageous network of interactions.

The Internet is a particularly fertile medium for the promotion of spontaneous interactions because it substantially reduces the information and transaction costs that limit the scope and sophistication of dealings in the physical world. In particular, the Internet greatly cuts the cost of information gathering. With the aid of a search engine, data can be collected from the various suppliers of a particular good or service operating anywhere in the world almost instantaneously and at minimal cost. The information collected can be extremely detailed, allowing consumers to expand the range of criteria that go to influence their choices. The process of selection from amongst alternatives may be largely or entirely automated with the aid of software agents, reducing transaction costs still further. It is improvements such as these which make e-commerce markets more 'frictionless' than their more conventional alternatives, lacking imperfections which would otherwise have impeded an efficient realisation of preferences. As well as enhancing the effectiveness of spontaneous transactions which take place across it, the Internet, in the manner of its own physical development, can itself be seen as a testament to the possibilities of spontaneous and diffuse collaboration. This 'network of networks' has grown through the interconnection of a patchwork of separate electronic communications networks, some public and some private, comprising a variety of technologies and transmission methods.

In the section of this contribution which immediately follows the introduction, we develop one practical example in support of the claim that the Internet's enhanced capacity for spontaneous interaction requires us to reconsider the necessity for state-imposed regulatory interventions to obtain socially valuable outcomes. Markets, when enhanced by the operation of the new communications technologies, may indeed achieve a great deal without the need for traditional vertical governance.

Some variants of the 'spontaneity' argument appear, however, to go much further and to suggest that the Internet is best kept free of all governmental intervention going beyond the minimal provision of a facilitative framework of private law rules, perhaps

H. Snijders, S. Weatherill (eds.), *E-commerce Law*, 93-103

supplemented by a framework of negative civil and political rights.[1] This approach to e-commerce regulation favours only such sectorspecific norms as are necessary to render viable individual transactions. On this view, both the identity of those transacting and the outcomes of their transactions fall outside the ambit of regulatory concern. Various strands can be distinguished at work in this type of approach.

First, a powerful rhetoric has emerged which represents the Internet as a zone of emancipation.[2] We have already identified one set of constraints from which the Internet might help to liberate transactions: namely, those imposed by physical location and limited information. However, often these types of constraint are elided with controls imposed by governments, which are also claimed to have less application in the online world. Some legal rules are said to be impossible to apply. Others have not yet been applied because of the newness of the medium. In any event, this escape from regulation is often regarded as an opportunity and a success.

Secondly, the spontaneity of the Internet may be favourably contrasted not only with traditional markets, but also with the outcomes of state activity. Here, an emphasis upon the spontaneous character of the Internet may come to intersect with a significant strand of economic liberal thinking, which conceives of the market as a self-constituting order, the strength of which lies in its capacity to process information more effectively than any central authority could hope to do. Consumers, in deciding how to commit their resources, are much the best placed to assess and prioritise amongst their own preferences. Producers, in planning how to invest their capital, are similarly better placed than any centralised public authority to measure, through the diffused and shifting signals of consumer demand, what consumers want. When public bodies do attempt to buck the market their informational disadvantage typically results in a wasteful misallocation of resources. Ideas about the spontaneity of the Internet therefore connect with ideas about the spontaneity of the market and seem to reinforce one another in forming a case against any but the most minimal regulatory intervention in e-commerce markets. The Internet is seen as impressive confirmation of the scope for unco-ordinated market interactions to result in extraordinarily complex and workable systems.[3]

---

1 For a representative example of this style of argument, see Peter Huber, *Law and Disorder in Cyberspace: Abolish the FCC and Let the Common Law Rule the Telecosm* (Oxford University Press, 1997). He argues (at p. 22) that 'the only prescription for meeting [the] heterogeneous and varied needs [of private individuals and corporations] is not to prescribe anything... The Web is probably the best model at hand... It is... an array of independently owned and managed networks, separately funded, separately developed, and separately maintained, with no single entity or agency in charge of managing everything'. At most, what is needed are 'laws to defend the property rights of people..., to enforce contracts and carriage agreements, to defend the freedom to speak and listen, and to protect copyright and privacy' (at p. 8).

2 On the freedom-enhancing potential of communications technologies, see Ithiel de Sola Pool, *Technologies of Freedom* (Harvard University Press, 1983). For an example of emancipatory rhetoric emphasising freedom from government, see Huber 1997, p. 206 (see note 1).

3 See Huber 1997, p. 8-9 (see note 1):
[Regulation by Commission] has failed. It is rigid, slow, and – despite all the earnest expertise of bureaucrats – ignorant. Market forces, mediated by common law, elicit information faster and more reliably. Markets constantly probe new technology, try out new forms of supply, and assess demand with a determination, precision and persistence that no commission can ever match... The Commission must go.'

By means of a second practical example, we aim to show that this approach is inadequate to maximise the spontaneity-enhancing features of the Internet. There is a role for public involvement in enabling a broad base of citizens to participate in the spontaneity of the Internet by promoting access to, and participation in, e-commerce markets. In pursuit of this objective, regulatory interventions need to go well beyond the provision of a facilitative framework of private law. They must build on a long tradition of promoting the provision of a universal service by the network-industries. However, because of the special features of the Internet, more flexible and creative solutions will have to be found than those which have traditionally been deployed to ensure widespread access to network technologies.

Our conclusions are therefore mixed. We express mitigated optimism at the novel potential for electronically enhanced markets to express altruistic or socially beneficent preferences through the consumption process itself. Such a possibility may be neglected by those who focus upon traditional top-down methods of securing desirable social outcomes. Also, however, we re-emphasise the importance of a broader infrastructural role for government, which becomes apparent once one begins to consider markets in their social context. Public facilitation of markets must be expanded beyond the scope of individual transactions, to encompass the provision of the means necessary to ensure widespread access to the particular advantages which accrue when markets and communications technologies are put together.

2 The social promise of spontaneously aggregated preferences

The social promise of a market order has always been mixed. On the positive side, the productive and allocative efficiency gains of spontaneity already mentioned are clearly socially desirable effects. On the other hand, the limitations of a market order in relation to outcomes like social cohesion and equality are also widely acknowledged. Indeed, a certain degree of 'social blindness' is implicit in the very concept of a self-constituting order that filters and aggregates individual preferences via a decentralised price mechanism. This 'social blindness' has two facets. First, the 'invisible hand' aspect of a market order means that there is no direct pursuit of collective goals beyond those of allocative efficiency: rather, such goals are the equivalent of the aggregate result of multiple individual preferences. Such aggregation is frequently insensitive to distributive concerns or to the production of externalities, negative outcomes the burden of which falls on parties beyond the scope of the immediate market transaction. Secondly, the abstraction of the price mechanism filters out knowledge about the terms and circumstances of production. While the price level stands as proxy for the value, including profits, of production inputs, there is in that proxy no direct information about the social context of that production.

Traditionally, these limitations of a market order have been considered remediable by either or both of two kinds of response: private charity, or state-imposed regulatory intervention (for example via the provision of public goods, or the operation of redistributive 'tax and spend' policies). Both private charity (notwithstanding its superficial connection with the notion of spontaneity) and state-imposed regulatory intervention are essentially administrative projects that pursue collective goals directly via bureaucratic direction or provision. As such, they sacrifice the efficiency gains that flow from the disaggregated, decentralised nature of a market. There is a real tension between this efficiency and the kind of socially beneficial outcome that requires consciously coordinated pursuit of certain substantive goals. Reflecting the obduracy of this tension, a large literature has developed exploring the promise held out by shifting from vertical to horizontal conceptions of governance.[4] Much of this literature, however, while it retreats somewhat from advocating top-down state-imposed regulatory intervention, still depends in many cases on an intermediate sense of vertical governance, where NGOs or insurance companies might take on functions formerly thought of as state functions. Horizontal tempering of market orders still involves governance, even if not always government. We suggest, however, that the technological dimension of e-commerce provides unexpected opportunities for socially beneficial outcomes to flow *directly* from the consumption choices of individual citizens, in ways that preserve the benefits of this devolved mode of aggregating preferences.

Udo Reifner, in a very interesting recent essay,[5] helps identify for us the specific feature of e-commerce that opens new opportunities for generating socially beneficial outcomes of a kind that are usually thought of as distorting the benefits of a market order. That feature is the fact that the technology of the Internet makes it possible to mark money with social preferences in a way that traditional markets have not been very good at. The abstraction of money is an important facet of the efficiency of a market order: the price of exchange is a proxy for a multitude of complex facts but money minimises the amount of information required to facilitate exchange. On the Internet, however, electronic money can be loaded with information, and then used with little or no additional cost at the level of individual transactions. This then means that money can transfer not just value but also information about *the source and purpose* of the value exchange. Just as 'dirty' money can already, under the auspices of money laundering regulation, be traced, identified, and channelled, so too could 'social money' in e-commerce. Social money might come to resemble an alternative currency, but without any of the attendant rigidities, limited scope and dubious legality.

Some examples can be drawn from existing sites on the web today. One version sells attention in such a way that individualised expressions of momentary concern for an issue translate directly into concrete social purposes or indirectly into money then channelled into social purposes. Www.thehungersite.com is an example of the former, where each click on a website publicising information about food shortages in various global regions links the 'clicker' to a commitment from a sponsor to

4 See for example Christine Parker's forthcoming exploration of a 'light-touch' government role in monitoring the self-regulatory activities of corporations in *The Open Corporation* (forthcoming Oxford University Press, 2002); Anne-Marie Slaughter's discussion of network governance at the international level in 'Agencies on the Loose? Holding Government Networks Accountable' in: George Bermann & Peter Lindseth (ed.), *Transatlantic Regulatory Cooperation*; Jody Freeman's support for 'collaborative governance' that self-consciously 'decentres the state' in 'The Private Role in Public Governance', *New York University Law Review* 75 (2000), p. 543-675.

5 Udo Reifner, 'The Lost Penny – Social Contract Law and Market Economy', in: Thomas Wilhelmsson and Samuli Hurri (eds.), *From Dissonance to Sense: Welfare State Expectations, Privatisation and Private Law* (Ashgate, 1999).

distribute food directly to those that need it. An example of the second is <www.give-water.org>, where clicks generate money that is used to provide the public good of water supplies for communities without such necessary luxuries. More developed examples actually sell goods or services rather than mere attention. 'Shop for Change', for example, allows purchasers of everyday items such as books or music CDs to utilise popular online retailers such as Amazon through a special portal that skims a certain percentage of the money spent for donation to social purposes. Moreover, the buyer can interact with the site in such a way as to refine his or her knowledge of the social and environmental impact of various retailers' business practices, and thereby participate in shaping their practices directly. As the website explains:

> Responsible shopping means taking into account the social and environmental impacts of your buying decisions. Our Responsible Shopper interactive database allows you to look up companies and determine their performance in a variety of categories while you are actually shopping or browsing on ShopForChange. It also includes overviews of the issues and positive alternatives in eleven product categories...
>
> Responsible Shopper can help you determine what types of products to purchase or avoid, what brands of the recommended product to buy, and which retailers to buy it from. It also allows you to send emails to these companies to give them praise for their records and to let them know why you have chosen to shop with them or to give them feedback on why you have chosen not to shop with them and/or to ask them to change their practices or procedures. Your buying decisions and feedback can have a profound impact.

<www.workingforchange.com/shop/responsibleshop.cfm>

A related website shows how the 'nested' feature of hyperlinked information on the Internet can thicken the socially loaded nature of transactions to the depth selected by the consuming individual. As www.responsibleshopper.org explains, 'for less familiar social or environmental issues, we provide context-sensitive help... which further explains the issue. Simply click on the icon and a page pops up with more information. If we failed to explain an issue clearly enough for you, please let us know. All information which comes from third parties (like a non-profit organisation or governmental agency) is attributed and includes a link to the source. In most cases these links lead directly to a page with more in-depth information on the issue.'

The point made by this provider about attribution brings our attention to a potential problem with this method of welding social concerns onto individual consumption, and that is possible fraud or misrepresentation in relation either to the use of any premium paid by the socially responsible consumer, or in relation to the information provided about the terms of production or the additional outcomes. Of course, this kind of fraud is equally possible in market settings not assisted by the Internet, and no less so in a world of mass consumption and arms-length contracting with impersonal strangers. However it does suggest an ongoing supervisory role for government in providing supportive infrastructure to guard against the possibility of fraud. This does not return us to traditional vertical governance, however. First, the intervention of government is not made in direct pursuit of particular social goals, but rather *indirectly facilitates* the pursuit of such goals. Secondly, drawing on the spirit of the literature on regulatory governance adverted to earlier, it would not necessarily have to be government that played this role. Benchmarking schemes, for example, that articulated standards for socially responsible consumption and monitored sites which promoted this could just as well be carried out by third party organisations with appropriate reputational capital in the eyes of those consumers participating in such schemes. For example, just as Shop for Change itself benchmarks existing online providers and provides an infrastructure that links to their market, so another public interest group could cross-check the information provided by Shop for Change and the uses made of the premium that Shop for Change extracts from the use of their online architecture.

We would even go so far as to argue that since individual consumers in this instance give their direct consent to 'social loading' at the level of each individual transaction, the monitoring of whether and how the social outcomes are provided does not, *relatively speaking*, raise legitimacy issues as urgently as legislatively mandated regulatory outcomes like minimum wages or tax-and-spend redistribution programmes. Consumers that *are* concerned to monitor can participate in the drafting of principles to ameliorate monitoring deficits for the socially responsible sub-communities in which they choose to participate on the web. Here again the minimal nature of transaction costs on the Internet is highly facilitative of a level of participation and self-governance that would be much more burdensome to achieve extra-technologically. The very plurality of benchmarking communities that may develop would itself serve as a system of 'checks and balances', or a background structure that provides for exit by disgruntled consumers, that would lessen again the need for top-down intervention. To ensure, however, that such sub-communities could gather electronically in reliable and trust-generating ways in the first place, one form of indirect facilitative regulation may be critically important: that of the provision of domain names. Here we already have an instance of a non-governmental body carrying out this function – the Internet Corporation for Assigned Names and Numbers (ICANN) – though the attendant criticisms currently being made of its lack of transparency and representativeness[6] highlight some of the problems that arise when horizontal governance focuses on highly salient, fundamentally constitutive issues.

The linked issues of insufficient representativeness and the possibility of exit from socially responsible online communities remind us of a further important problem which we do not wish to appear to ignore: that of free-riding. While redistribution raises problems of fraud more acutely, some of the desirable social outcomes welded onto online consumption choices relate more to non-excludable public goods and these can easily be free-ridden. Given their importance, we might, as a community, not want to rely on individual acts of altruism, but rather insist that people by majoritarian means pre-commit themselves to a particular, socially desirable course. In respect of this, we emphasise that the promise that we see in this aspect of the 'spontaneous' region of e-commerce is *supplementary to*, not substitutive of, state-based redistribution and provision of public goods. The efficiency problems and threats to autonomy associated with 'vertical' governance make these strategies second-best and they have suffered politically in recent decades in consequence. Socially loaded

6 See for example Michael Froomkin, 'A Wrong Turn in Cyberspace: Using Icann to Route Around the APA and the Constitution', *Duke Law Journal* 50 (2000), 17-186; Jonathan Weinberg, 'Icann and the Problem of Legitimacy' *Duke Law Journal* 50 (2000) 187-260.

money, in facilitating socially or environmentally preferred preference direction *at the level of the individual transaction*, to an extent ameliorates one of the classic barriers to collective action: the absence of a tangible quid pro quo for the social contribution of the individual member. Thus the 'social' meaning of money in the e-commerce context can be *built into the internal structure* of commercial exchange at an individualised level, rather than being performed separately by administrative projects whether of a private charitable or a government nature.

Socially responsible e-commerce that depends on networks of consumers rather than networks of state officials with a specific mandate is at the very least worth considering as an important gloss on the 'socially blind' market. We raise it to point to some of the creative possibilities that could emerge in e-commerce, building on the strengths of ways in which groups of individuals via technology, rather than the state, can shape the otherwise socially random interrelation of preferences in a market. If there is even some partial way in which individuals can *themselves* define what should be social, thus thickening the content of 'social' via aggregated individual demand rather than collective substantive consensus, it seems an attractive promise in societies where it is increasingly difficult to secure that kind of substantive consensus on values or goals. The promise of spontaneity here, if fulfilled, would give market power more of the character of a democratic vote. To the sceptics at this point, we urge a pause, however, because the points made in the next section are crucial to the persuasiveness of this aspect of spontaneity's promise.

3 The peril of spontaneity: inaccessible Internet-assisted markets

Thus far, we have sought to demonstrate that the enhancement of spontaneity attainable by e-commerce markets does indeed require us to rethink our understanding of the respective roles of vertical and horizontal governance. However, we want to resist the stronger conclusions which some have derived from the spontaneous character of the Internet: that governmental intervention can now be limited to the provision of a facilitative framework of private law rules. We intend to focus here on the need for broader regulatory intervention in order to ensure widespread access to the benefits of online interactions. If the distribution of Internet access is left to develop in a spontaneous pattern, it may come to compound the disadvantage of groups already suffering exclusion. The significant promise of spontaneity online necessitates careful and creative policy making to ensure that it does not only enhance the life chances of those already rich in options.

As a starting point it should be remembered that in all markets, public authorities have come to play a vital role in determining the ambit of transaction through what we might term 'infrastructural' regulation. Physical networks are crucial in expanding and thereby improving the efficiency of markets. Regional policy is therefore typically heavily associated with the strategic design of transport networks.

The concern of policy makers has traditionally been directed not only at widening markets for purely efficiency-related reasons, but also at producing a more equitable spread of economic opportunities. Where people are located on the transport, communications and energy networks is a crucial determinant of their ability to benefit from the operation of markets. In the traditional network industries (gas, electricity, transport, water, post and telecommunications), universal service policies have involved the provision of standardised tariffs. These have applied despite the higher cost of serving consumers who make less use of the networks in question because of their low income, or who are more expensive to serve because of their rural location. When such networks were operated by state monopolies, they were funded through an elaborate system of cross-subsidies. Since liberalisation, funding has often come instead from a universal levy upon all service providers. The establishment of universal service policies in relation to essential network services reflects the strongly felt need to equalise opportunities for market access.

In light of this long regulatory tradition, apparent in both the USA and Europe, it is unsurprising that attempts have been made to develop policies aimed at ensuring fair access to the new communications medium of the Internet. Reference to the risk of a digital divide is now all too familiar. Policy documents repeat like a mantra the need for policies targeted at avoiding social exclusion from the economic potentialities opened up by the Internet.

However, powerful arguments have been raised against attempts to devise universal service policies applicable to the Internet. These arguments advocate the desirability of spontaneous expansion of Internet usage, according to the preferences of consumers expressed in the market. Thus, first, it is argued against any attempt to subsidise the development of broadband networks that such a policy would involve backing particular technologies, giving them an artificial and market-distorting advantage over existing or potential rivals. However, it is asserted, public authorities have proven to be very bad at picking winners. The consequence of their efforts is often to entrench expensive and obsolescent technologies, dampening the inherent incentive in a free market to find innovative and cost-saving solutions.[7] Better, therefore, to leave markets to develop the infrastructure of the Internet, without attempting to force the roll-out of networks, even for reasons of equity.

A second argument which is advanced against any extension of universal service to the Internet contends that such an intervention would result in an over-allocation of resources to the new technologies. In part, this objection may be based simply on a belief in consumer sovereignty: for the state to invest more in goods or services than consumers in the market have themselves chosen to do is viewed as an impermissible exercise in paternalism. More subtly, it may be argued, even by those who accept that the state should sometimes invest in merit goods for the good of its citizens, that funding for an expansion of Internet access should not be derived from universal service charges levies upon traditional telephony. To do so would be to reduce the cost of the new services, enjoyed by a tiny (and already privileged) fraction of the population, whilst forcing up the price of plain old telecommunications ser-

---

7 DSL technologies, which use digital compression technologies to increase the bandwidth of existing copper wire telephone lines, provide a good example of the market operating to generate new and affordable options. Prior to the emergence of these technologies, if governments had chosen to invest heavily in creating a high capacity fibre network, they would have committed significantly more resources than was necessary to the task of providing widespread high speed Internet access.

vices, although these latter services are much more highly valued by the majority of users.

Finally, it may be argued that access to network infrastructure is in itself of little value given the basket of other endowments which consumers need to make proper use of it. Thus, access to a network will not avail a user without a computer terminal to attach to it. Without a significant deployment of resources, the state could not hope to supply every household, let alone every citizen, with a computer. Any such initiative would, anyway, again involve the state in artificially entrenching a particular technological solution. Similarly, a major educational initiative would be required to ensure the necessary levels of computer literacy. Even then, e-commerce would only become a possibility if citizens had access to credit card facilities of a kind still denied to many so as to allow them to make payments online. Given that these various endowments would currently be expensive and difficult for the state to confer across a broad cross-section of the population, it is more practical to wait for the market to develop at its own speed.

Such arguments usefully highlight a number of potential pitfalls in the design of policies to broaden access to the Internet. However, they do not present a convincing case against attempts to adapt universal service policies to the new communications technologies. At most the first argument shows the need to adopt technology-neutral policies, which promote access across a number of technological platforms. The first version of the second argument ignores the important contribution which every state makes to the purchase of merit goods. It also neglects the positive network externalities which may result to all users from an expansion in network penetration. Insofar as the second version of the second argument has merit, it can be met by drawing financial support for policies designed to broaden access to the Internet from some source other than traditional telephone services. The third argument also goes to means rather than ends, demonstrating the difficulty of the task, but not undermining its value.

This is not to say that a careful balancing exercise is not required when deciding at what stage it becomes worthwhile to commit significant resources to extending Internet access, given the other pressing calls upon the public purse. If the Internet does indeed enhance people's capacity to constitute spontaneous networks of interaction than would traditionally have been possible offline, the provision of widespread access, and the cultivation of skills to make use of that access, would assume some importance. They would appear to be a good example of the state operating to enable its citizens, modifying the spontaneous distribution of opportunity precisely in order to extend the sphere within which spontaneous transactions can then occur.

To be sure, because the challenges of access are multi-layered, and not limited to access to the network infrastructure, public action would necessarily involve a wide range of initiatives. Moreover, it would entail a substantial degree of collaboration between public and private actors, the state encouraging and supporting action by computer manufacturers, network operators, service providers and banks to enable a wider range of users to utilise the new technologies effectively. Moreover, there may be scope for precisely the types of socially responsible consumption choices which we have discussed above. When choosing between Internet service providers, some users might wish to select an organisation which manifested a commitment to promoting access by, for example, making free terminals available in schools or public libraries. In any event, a more varied pattern of interaction between public and private actors appears more likely to achieve results than the more traditional top down approaches which have in the past gone to advance universal service in the network industries.

4 CONCLUSION

We have suggested here that e-commerce provides a qualitatively novel context for thinking through long-familiar tensions between the promise and peril of spontaneous interaction. The novelty of this context provides grounds for a qualified optimism towards new ways of combining different modes of governance in the pursuit of socially optimal outcomes. To some degree, the perils raised in the second section are very familiar ones, debated in not dissimilar terms across the longue duree of the welfare state. Along this trajectory, gradually more goods and services have acquired sufficiently central roles in collective life, such that social cohesion depends on a minimal level of universal access to them. But what is new about the Internet as an essential service is that it is not so much a *precondition* for effective participation in social settings (including markets), but it *is itself* a zone of participation, a social setting where agency and autonomy can flourish. For this reason, policies that promote access to the Internet have more promise of establishing linkages with spontaneous modes of social interaction, and are perhaps less subject to the concerns about paternalism that state-imposed regulatory intervention so often brings in its train. There is thus a synergy between improved access and the benefits of spontaneity that is particularly strong in the context of the Internet, with the consequence that the unexpected promise of 'socially loaded' individual transactions can be significantly magnified by improved access.

In tandem with the qualified optimism about the substantive aspects of the Internet as a novel zone of commerce come provisional views that traditional top-down modes of governance are neither necessary nor appropriate in such a setting, while at the same time, 'pure spontaneity' is equally undesirable. While this contribution is a preliminary conceptualisation of key issues, and stops well short of developing detailed proposals for governing e-commerce, we would suggest that any approach to establishing a regulatory framework for e-commerce should build initially upon broad principles. Such principles could be binding in the context of access but non-binding in case of providing supportive infrastructure for socially responsible consumption frameworks. An example of the former might be the community principle in the proposed EU Charter for Fundamental Rights that ensures the supply of general interest services; the latter could be embodied in a Model Code drawing on principles of benchmarking organisations that monitor the outcomes of socially responsible consumption patterns. John Braithwaite has recently argued[8] that empirically speaking there is evidence to indicate that in complex actions in

8 John Braithwaite, *Rules and Principles: A Theory of Legal Certainty*, Paper delivered to Australian Society of Legal Philosophy Conference (Australian National University, June 2001).

changing environments where large economic interests are at stake, governance by reference to relatively few numbers of diffuse principles actually promotes not only better deliberation but also, perhaps counter-intuitively, more certainty. We suggest that in addition to these benefits, the use of broad principles would also provide the limited constraints on spontaneity for which we have argued, while still leaving space for institutional experimentation with different mixes of horizontal and vertical governance strategies. In this way, we may defuse problems that could otherwise imperil the promise of spontaneity proffered by e-commerce.

The database right and the spin-off theory

Dirk Visser

1 Introduction

For the time being, information is the only commodity that can be transferred electronically. Therefore, information, especially large quantities of valuable information contained in databases, is the (only) ideal object for electronic commerce. Information contained in databases cannot only be bought and sold, but can also be actually delivered over the Internet. At the same time, valuable information contained in databases can also be copied and transferred over the Internet without any permission or control of the person or persons who have invested substantially in this information.

Therefore, a certain degree of protection of databases forms the very core of the success of trading information over the Internet. The overprotection of databases could on the other hand be a serious impediment to the development of electronic commerce. If too much protection is granted, unjustified information monopolies may arise, which may make it impossible for new players to come onto the electronic marketplace.

In 1996 the European Database Directive came into force which introduced a new pseudo-copyright in databases.[1] This Directive was implemented in the Netherlands in 1999, in the Databases (Legal Protection) Act [*Databankenwet]* of July 8, 1999[2] and in the UK in 1997, in The Copyright and Rights in Databases Regulations 1997.[3] The most important paragraph of the Database Directive is article 7:

> Member States shall provide for a right for the maker of a database which shows that there has been qualitatively and/or quantitatively a substantial investment in either the obtaining, verification or presentation of the contents to prevent extraction and/or re-utilization of the whole or of a substantial part, evaluated qualitatively and/or quantitatively, of the contents of that database' (art. 7 Database Directive).

The definition of this new right contains quite a few vague notions. The requirement for protection is: a *qualitatively and/or quantitatively substantial* investment. The criterion for infringement is (extraction and/or re-utilization of the whole or of) a *qualitatively and/or quantitatively substantial* part of the contents of that database.

1 Directive 96/9/EC of the European Parliament and of the Council of 11 March 1996 on the legal protection of databases, Official Journal No. L 77 of 27 March 1996, p. 20.
2 Stb. 1999, 303.
3 SI 1997 no. 3032.

H. Snijders, S. Weatherill (eds.), *E-commerce Law*, 105-110

2 SPIN-OFF THEORY

In the course of the parliamentary debate on the implementation of the Database Directive in Dutch law, the following question was posed to the Minister of Justice concerning the meaning of the wording 'substantial investment':

> Furthermore, the members of the PvdA (= labour) party wonder whether the 'substantial investment' mentioned in this definition [of a protected database] must (primarily) be directed at the obtaining, verification or presentation of the database in question. In explanation of this question the members give the following three examples:
>
> 1. The yearly award of Michelin stars to restaurants does with doubt require a substantial investment and results in the Netherlands in a very small collection of data, a list of around ten names and addresses of restaurants and the number of stars they have. The investment seems, however, primarily directed at the awarding of stars, not at the obtaining of a short list of names and addresses of restaurants. Is such a list of ten restaurants with a Michelin star in the Netherlands a protected database?
> 2. The discovery of a new solar system requires a substantial investment in a telescope or a journey into space. It results, among other things, in the obtaining of a collection of stars with their given names. Is such a collection a protected database?
> 3. The compilation of the programming schedule of a television channel does probably require a substantial investment and results in a collection of data, the programming data. The investment involved is, however, without doubt primarily directed at the broadcasting of the programmes at particular, expressly chosen times. The collection of programming data is in fact not much more than a spin-off of the scheduling of the programmes of the channel. Can it be said in such a case that the collection of data as such shows that there has been a substantial investment that qualifies for protection?
>
> The members of the PvdA party are aware [...] of the fact that these questions must eventually be answered in European case law, but they are of the opinion that these questions are of such fundamental importance, that at least an effort must be made to try to answer these questions.

The Minister of Justice gave the following answers to these questions:

> According to the definition [of a protected database] the substantial investment can be either in the obtaining or the verification or in the presentation of the contents of a database. In the case of the short list of restaurants with a Michelin star, the investment is indeed, as the members themselves already remark, directed at the awarding of the stars and not at the obtaining of the short list. This is enough reason for this short list not to be considered a database within the meaning of the [Databases (Legal Protection) Act [*Databankenwet*]] Act. On top of that, one may well ask whether such a short list can be considered a *collection* of data. It does in fact contain only one fact. A collection of stars -probably what is meant is a list in which the newly discovered stars are mentioned with their names – shall for the same reason not fall within the definition of a [protected] database. The investment is concerned with the research through a telescope or space journey. Furthermore, here also one might well ask whether the resulting short list must be considered a collection of data. If programming data are indeed, as these members suppose, no more than a spin-off of the scheduling of the programmes of the channel, the substantial investment which is necessary in order for the programming data to fall under the definition of a database will be lacking. Whether that is the case, and if so, what consequences this has for the applicability of this bill, is a matter which has to be decided by the courts on the basis of the actual facts of the case.

These questions and answers probably form the basis of the so-called spin-off theory: the theory that in order for a database to be protected under the sui-generis right there must be proof of a substantial investment directed at the obtaining, verification or presentation of the database in question. If the investment was directed at another activity, and the database is merely a spin-off of this other activity, this investment should not be taken into account.

3 TELEPHONE DIRECTORIES

Before the implementation of the database Directive the spin-off argument was brought before the Court of Appeal at Arnhem in the KPN/Denda-case[4] concerning the protectability of telephone directories. The defendant Denda argued that the collection of telephone directory data was merely a spin-off of its main activity as telephone operator and that a substantial investment in the database as such was lacking. The Court of Appeal rejected this argument, stating that the Directive does not distinguish between primary and secondary exploitations of databases as suggested by Denda. In the follow-up of the KPN/Denda-case the spin-off argument has subsequently also been rejected by the District Court of Almelo.[5]

In relation to telephone directories the spin-off argument has also been rejected by the President of the District Court at The Hague in the KPN/XSO-case.[6]

> The Court is of the opinion that the fact that KPN for its main activities has to have at its disposal in some form the data that is contained in its electronic and paper copy telephone directories does not preclude the applicability of the Database Act, not only because it can be assumed that also for the presentation of the database in a way which makes it accessible for the general public (on the internet, on CD-ROM) considerable expenses have been made and are still being made, but also because there is no reason why the substantial investment that KPN has made and keeps on making in these databases should be excluded from protection which the Database Directive has introduced explicitly for the benefit of investments in databases, for no other reason than that this investment would also have been made if this protection had not existed.

4 PROGRAMMING DATA

In its decision of 10 September 1998 the Netherlands Competition Authority (NMA) considered the following regarding the protection of programming data under the database sui generis right:

> It is questionable whether [the broadcasting organisations] make substantial investments as meant by the Directive in order to make the programming schedules. As mentioned above, programming schedules are indeed a by-product of the scheduling of the programmes. It cannot be assumed that the obtaining of programming schedules involves more than the input of the results of the scheduling in a computer.

In his decision of 3 October 2001[7] the Director-General of the Netherlands Competi-

4 Court of Appeal Arnhem 15 April 1997, AMI (1997), p. 214, *Mediaforum* 1997, p. 72.
5 District Court Almelo 6 December 2000, AMI (2001), p. 69 note Cohen Jehoram, *Mediaforum*.
6 President District Court The Hague 14 January 2000, AMI (2000), p. 71 note Beunen at p. 58, *Mediaforum* (2000), p. 64 note Hugenholtz, IER (2000), p. 73 note Grosheide, *Computerrecht* (2000), p. 154 note Aalberts and Schellekens.
7 D-g Nma 3 October 2002, *Mediaforum* (2002), p. 69.

tion Authority (NMA) seems to have agreed with the opinion of the Advisory Committee on Appeal of 27 June 2000 (in par. 106):[8]

> The sui generis right of this [Database Directive] does not apply. Because the programming schedules are only a by-product of the programme scheduling process, no substantial investment has taken place in it.

On 30 January 2001[9] the Court of Appeal in The Hague ruled that the Netherlands Broadcasting Corporation (NOS) had not proven that a substantial investment had taken place in the making of the programming schedules:

> Moreover, the broadcasting organisations, whose primary task it is to take care of national radio and television broadcasting, cannot perform this task without compiling programming data and making programming schedules, in which, while the contrary has not been proven, it must be assumed that with the mere making of the programming schedules no (separate) substantial investment is made, in time, money or otherwise. The Court finds support for its view in the position taken by the Minister of Justice, from which it follows that a substantial investment may be lacking if television programming data is no more than a spin-off of the programming of the channel.

The Dutch Broadcasters have appealed against this decision at the Supreme Court (Hoge Raad). A decision is not to be expected before the summer of 2003.

5 Real estate information

National newspaper De Telegraaf under the name of El Cheapo offered a search service for real estate on the Internet, using, amongst others, the real estate database of NVM and presented the results in its own format with deep links to the original NVM pages. NVM is the largest association of real estate agents in the Netherlands. NVM brought a case against De Telegraaf in summary proceedings. The President of the The Hague District Court ruled that the real estate database of NVM was protected by the database right and that the activity of De Telegraaf constituted an infringement thereof.

The Court of Appeal in The Hague, however, was of the opinion that the real estate database of NVM was not protected by the database right, because the database had not originally been intended for use on the Internet:[10]

> It is unlikely that the amount as stated in the exhibit was directed at the obtaining, verification or presentation of the database on the Internet. Further, no documents have been submitted to the Court on the basis of which it can be assumed that a substantial investment has been made directed at the obtaining, verification or presentation of the database on the Internet. Besides, the Court of Appeal has considered the point of view of the Minister of Justice, from which it can be deduced that a substantial investment can be lacking when the data of the database constitutes no more than a spin-off of the main activity or another activity of the producer.

---

8 Advisory Committee on Appeal of 27 June 2000, <www.nma-org.nl.>

9 Court of Appeal The Hague 30 January 2002, AMI (2001), p. 73 note Cohen Jehoram.

10 Court of Appeal The Hague 21 December 2000, AMI (2001), p. 71 note Cohen Jehoram.

On 22 March 2002 the Supreme Court of the Netherlands (Hoge Raad) reversed the decision of the Court of Appeal of The Hague:[11]

> The Court of Appeal has taken into account that a substantial investment can be lacking when the data of the database are not more than a 'spin-off' of the main activity or another activity of the producer. The Court of Appeal has applied article 1 under a of the Databases (Legal Protection) Act [*Databankenwet*] wrongly in considering of decisive importance proof of a substantial investment directed at the obtaining, verification or presentation of the database on the Internet. Neither the text nor the meaning of this clause impels us not to take into consideration the investment that has been made directed at the collection and arrangement of the data, apart from the question whether and when this data will be put on the Internet. Also, the spin-off argument of the Court of Appeal, derived from a statement of the Minister of Justice at the parliamentary proceedings of the Databankenwet, is meaningless in this context, since neither the Directive nor the text of article 1 under a of the Databankenwet leads to the view that, in case a database is used for different purposes, it is necessary to point out a substantial investment for each purpose separately. Besides, the view of the Court of Appeal would lead to considerable difficulties regarding the delineation. Even when it is correct that the data of the database was already directed at the main activities of the estate agents, it is still possible that the database, when it is made available to the public by means of the Internet, qualifies for protection on the basis of the Directive or the Databankenwet.

In the reporting of this case in several newsletters and in comments on this decision, it has been suggested that the Supreme Court has clearly rejected the so-called spin-off theory.

It is important however, to note that the Supreme Court argued that 'the spin-off argument [...], is meaningless **in this context**, since neither the Directive nor the text of article 1 under a of the Databankenwet leads to the view that, in case a database is used for different purposes, it is necessary to point out a substantial investment for each purpose separately'[emphasis added].

It can be argued that the Supreme Court has not rejected the possibility that the required substantial investment might be lacking if no substantial investment directed at the compilation of any database (for any purpose) has taken place and a database is indeed just a spin-off of another activity, not being the compilation of any database as such. This may, for instance, be the case with the aforementioned programming data.

6 Sports betting data

Outside the Netherlands some interesting database decisions have been rendered in the field of sports betting data. In Sweden, the Gotland City Court ruled that the information relating to soccer matches did not constitute a protected database.[12] In the United Kingdom, the High Court (Laddie J.) ruled that the database with information on horseracing did constitute a protected database and that the copying of the

11 Supreme Court 22 March 2002, AMI (2002), p. 88 note Visser, IER (2002), p. 150 note Speyart.

12 Gotland City Court, 11 April 2000. *Fixtures Marketing Ltd.* v. *AB Svenska Spel*, mentioned in the Court of Appeal decision in William Hill.

most recent information was an infringing extraction of a substantial part.[13] The Court of Appeal did, however, find it necessary to pose questions to the European Court of Justice,[14] but these questions have not been actually referred to the Court of Justice as yet.

In Finland, the District Court of Vantaa also had to decide a case on betting information for soccer matches.[15] This Court on 1 February 2002 referred the following questions to the Court of Justice:[16]

> 1. May the requirement in Article 7(1) of the Directive for a link between the investment and the making of the database be interpreted in the sense that the 'obtaining' referred to in Article 7(1) and the investment directed at it refers, in the present case, to investment which is directed at the determination of the dates of the matches and the match pairings themselves, and, when the criteria for granting protection are appraised, does the drawing up of the fixture list include investment which is not relevant?
>
> 2. Is the object of the Directive to provide protection in such a way that persons other than the authors of the fixture list may not, without authorisation, use the data in that fixture list for betting or other commercial purposes?
>
> 3. For the purposes of the Directive, does the use by Veikkaus relate to a substantial part, evaluated qualitatively and/or quantitatively, of the database, having regard to the fact that, of the data in the fixture list, on each occasion only data necessary for one week is used in the weekly pools coupons, and that the fact that the data relating to the matches is obtained and verified from sources other than the maker of the database continuously throughout the season?

The first question posed by the Finnish Court will probably put the spin-off theory to the test at the European level. The other two questions are also of considerable importance for the development of the database sui-generis right in Europe.

---

13 High Court of Justice 9 February 2001, *British Horseracing Board* v. *William Hill*, Case No. HC 2000 1335.

14 Court of Appeal, 31 July 2001.

15 District Court of Vantaa,1 February 2002, *Fixtures Marketing Ltd* v. *OY Veikkaus Ab.*

16 European Court of Justice Case nr C-46/02.

E-commerce and private international law

Robert Stevens

This contribution will attempt to discuss the specific problems which e-commerce gives rise to in the context of private international law. It may be speculated that difficulties may arise both in relation to deciding whether a court has jurisdiction and, if it has, as to which law it will apply.

1 Jurisdiction

In England, and other European countries, there are two parallel systems of civil jurisdiction. Until recently these were the Brussels/Lugano Conventions[1] and the traditional national law rules. Following the Treaty of Amsterdam[2] responsibility for private international law has been assumed by the European Commission. The Brussels/Lugano Conventions were superseded on 1 March 2002 by Council Regulation No 44/2001[3] on jurisdiction and enforcement of judgements in civil and commercial matters. The United Kingdom and Ireland, who had a choice, decided to adopt the Regulation. Denmark is not bound by this Regulation under the Treaty of Amsterdam. The Hague Conference Preliminary Draft Convention on Jurisdiction and Foreign Judgments in Civil and Commercial Matters[4] follows a similar structure to the Regulation. The Regulation follows the general approach of the Conventions but differs in some important respects. I will base my discussion on the Regulation and only mention the Conventions where they differed.

Only if the Regulation has no application or delegates jurisdiction to the national law will the national rules be applicable. The English national rules can give rise to internet related problems. For purposes of obtaining jurisdiction, it may be necessary to decide where a contract was made or was broken.[5] I will confine my discussion to the Regulation.

---

1 Respectively these are the Convention on Jurisdiction and the Enforcement of Judgments in Civil and Commercial Matters 1968 (Brussels Convention) [1972] OJ L299/32 and The Convention on Jurisdiction and Enforcement of Judgments in Civil and Commercial Matters 1988 (Lugano Convention) [1988] OJ L319/9.

2 Treaty of Amsterdam amending the Treaty on European Union, the Treaties establishing the European Communities and certain related acts [1997] OJ C340/115.

3 Council Regulation (EC) No 44/2001 of 22 December 2000 on jurisdiction and the recognition and enforcement of judgments in civil and commercial matters (Regulation 44/2001) [2001] OJ L12/1.

4 Preliminary Draft Convention on Jurisdiction and Foreign Judgments in Civil and Commercial Matters (30/10/1999).

5 Civil Procedure Rules 1998, r 6.20(5), (6).

H. Snijders, S. Weatherill (eds.), *E-commerce Law*, 111-116

The Regulation applies, generally speaking, in civil and commercial matters.[6] The general rule is that persons domiciled in a Member State shall, whatever their nationality, be sued in the courts of that Member State.[7] If the defendant is not domiciled in a Member State then, generally, the national rules apply.

This general rule is, however, subject to exceptions. For example, the English courts may have exclusive jurisdiction regardless of domicile if the proceedings have as their object rights in rem in immovable property or tenancies of immovables situated within England.[8] Most of these exceptions do not, however, give rise to problems specific to e-commerce.

Consumers

Business-to Business dealings do not seem to give rise to problems specific to e-commerce. Business-to-Consumer dealings may. In relation to the specified consumer contracts, a consumer has the choice whether to sue in the courts of the place of his domicile or in the courts of the place where the other party is domiciled.[9] The other party is given no such choice and must proceed in the courts of the consumer's domicile.[10]

The relevant consumer contracts are defined by article 15:

> *Article 15*
> 1. In matters relating to a contract concluded by a person, the consumer, for a purpose which can be regarded as being outside his trade or profession, jurisdiction shall be determined by this Section, ..., if:
>   (a) it is a contract for the sale of goods on instalment credit terms; or
>   (b) it is a contract for a loan repayable by instalments, or for any other form of credit, made to finance the sale of goods; or
>   (c) in all other cases, the contract has been concluded with a person who pursues commercial or professional activities in the Member State of the consumer's domicile or, by any means, directs such activities to that Member State or to several States including that Member State, and the contract falls within the scope of such activities.

This article differs from the Brussels/Lugano Conventions in two important respects. The most important categories of contract are covered by art. 15(1)(c). The Regulation now covers those cases where the business *directs such activities to that Member State or to several States including that Member State, and the contract falls within the scope of such activities.* The Brussels/Lugano Conventions formerly required that in the State of the consumer's domicile (a) the conclusion of the contract was preceded by a specific invitation addressed to him or by advertising, and (b) the consumer

6 Article 1.1.
7 Article 2.
8 Article 22.1.
9 Article 16.1.
10 Article 16.2.

took the steps necessary for the conclusion of the contract.[11] The removal of (b) may have been thought necessary as it might be difficult to ascertain, where a contract has been concluded over the internet, precisely where the steps necessary for conclusion were taken. A difficult question, which no longer arises under the Regulation, is whether a 'webvertisement' would be advertising within a Member State.

Does an internet business which sells to consumers within a Member State 'direct' its activities at that Member State within the meaning of the Regulation? The answer seems obscure. Arguably a company which is prepared to sell to consumers who request good or services over the internet directs its activities at all Member States into which it is prepared to sell or supply. The Commission in its response to the European Parliament's proposal for amendments to the draft Regulation stated that 'the very existence of [a consumer contract] would seem to be a clear indication that a supplier of the goods or services has directed his activities to the state where the consumer is domiciled'.[12] If this is correct then in virtually all cases of consumer contracts concluded using the world wide web the consumer is given the protection of article 16. It may be that sales from a website the language of which is Dutch are not 'directed' at consumers domiciled in England, the number of English domiciled consumers who are able to read Dutch is not significant. However, it must be very doubtful whether a website the language of which is English could be said to be directed only at consumers domiciled in the United Kingdom and Ireland.

Alternatively, it might be argued that unless the business has actively marketed itself in some way, junk email ('spam') for example, a 'passive' website should not be seen as being directed at any particular Member State. This does not seem to be a plausible interpretation.

Clearly, the protection afforded to consumers both in relation to the courts in which they may be sued and in which they may choose to sue is extensive. For the small or medium sized business which decides to offer goods or services internationally over the internet in a way not previously practically possible, the possiblity of litigation in a country the legal system of which is alien is a real one. Even if consumer protection rules were to be harmonised throughout the European Union the prospects of resolving a dispute in a foreign country with unknown legal procedures would be a significant concern for businesses. Some businesses may, therefore, respond by restricting the class of European Union consumers they are prepared to contract with to those domiciled in either their own jurisdiction or one they feel confident of litigating in.

Tort

Under article 5.3 a person domiciled in a Member State may be sued in another Member State where in matters relating to tort delict or quasi-delict, in the place

11 Lugano Convention Art. 13.3.

12 Amended proposal for a Council Regulation on jurisdiction and the recognition and enforcement of judgments in civil and commercial matters (presented by the Commission pursuant to article 250 (2) of the EC-Treaty) [2002] OJ C062/E at para. 2.2.2.

where the harmful event occurred or may occur. This provision is substantially the same as the equivalent within the Brussels/Lugano Convention.[13] The concept of the 'place of the harmful event' was considered in *Shevill* v. *Press Alliance*.[14] The plaintiffs wished to commence proceedings in England in respect of a libel published in a French newspaper with a very small circulation in England. The court held that the courts of each Contracting State where the publication was distributed and where the plaintiff claimed to have suffered loss of reputation, will have jurisdiction to rule solely in respect of the harm caused in the State of the court seised. The Court also held that it is for the substantive law applicable to determine the existence and extent of the harm. The House of Lords applying this rule held that where English law presumes that the publication of a defamatory statement is harmful to the person defamed without specific proof of damage, that is sufficient for article 5(3).[15]

Where words are published on a web page, the potential for a court to take jurisdiction in proceedings appears to be very wide. The court of any Member State where the words are read may potentially be able to take jurisdiction.

2 Applicable Law

The choice of law rules in contract for the English courts (and the courts of other contracting states) are now to be found in the provisions of the Convention on the Law Applicable to Contractual Obligations ('the Rome Convention')[16] enacted into English law by the Contracts (Applicable Law) Act 1990. Two protocols exist to confer jurisdiction on the European Court of Justice to provide interpretive readings of the Convention.[17] They are not, however, yet in force. The parties to the contract are free to choose the law governing most contractual issues.[18] In the absence of choice, which law will govern? Under article 4.2 it is presumed that the contract is governed by the place of the habitual residence of the party rendering characteristic performance.

Again, it is in relation to Business-to-Consumer dealings where problems in relation to e-commerce may arise.

Article 5 provides, inter alia:

> 1. This Article applies to a contract the object of which is the supply of goods or services to a person ('the consumer') for a purpose which can be regarded as being outside his trade or profession, or a contract for the provision of credit for that object.

---

13 Article 5.3.

14 [1995] ECR I-415.

15 *Shevill* v. *Presse Alliance SA* [1996] AC 959 (HL).

16 Convention on the Law Applicable to Contractual Obligations opened for signature in Rome on 19 June 1980 ('Rome Convention') [1980] OJ L266/1.

17 These are the First and Second Protocols on the interpretation by the Court of Justice of the European Communities of the Convention on the law applicable to contractual obligations, opened for signature in Rome on 19 June 1980 [1989] L48/1; [1989] OJ L48/17 respectively.

18 Article 3.

2. Notwithstanding the provisions of Article 3, a choice of law made by the parties shall not have the result of depriving the consumer of the protection afforded to him by the mandatory rules of the law of the country in which he has his habitual residence:
   - if in that country the conclusion of the contract was preceded by a specific invitation addressed to him or by advertising, and he had taken in that country all the steps necessary on his part for the conclusion of the contract, or

   ...
3. Notwithstanding the provisions of Article 4, a contract to which this Article applies shall, in the absence of choice in accordance with Article 3, be governed by the law of the country in which the consumer has his habitual residence if it is entered into in the circumstances described in paragraph 2 of this Article.
4. This Article shall not apply to:
   (a) a contract of carriage;
   (b) a contract for the supply of services where the services are to be supplied to the consumer *exclusively in a country other than that in which he has his habitual residence.*

The concern for the business offering goods or services to customers over the web is that they may be subject to consumer protection rules they do not and cannot be reasonably expected to know. A choice of law clause will not protect them if the contract falls within article 5. Article 5 seems most likely to apply where in the country of the consumer's habitual residence 'the conclusion of the contract was preceded by a specific invitation addressed to [the consumer] or by advertising, and he had taken in that country all the steps necessary on his part for the conclusion of the contract'. Clearly an email sent to a consumer soliciting business would be covered but are 'webverts'? At the time of drafting the internet did not significantly exist. It might be argued that webverts should be covered.[19] The supplier must be aware of the potential reach of his website and might be said to take the risk of the mandatory rules of a consumer's habitual residence overriding his choice of law. However, the commentators on the Rome Convention, Giuliano & Lagarde,[20] state that there must be an intention to advertise in a Member State, an advertisement in an American edition of an American publication would not be an advertisement in Germany even if copies were sold in Germany. Such a restrictive approach makes little sense in relation to webverts.

The wording of the protection for consumers contained within article 5 of the Rome Convention is virtually identical to that which applied under the Brussels/ Lugano Conventions in matters of jurisdiction. This was clearly convenient and it is unfortunate that the rules on jurisdiction and choice of law now require separate analysis.

It may be noted in passing that the Directive on the protection of consumers in 'distance contracts'[21] does not include within the indicative list of 'distance selling techniques' sales via websites. The United Kingdom has not yet enacted this directive.

---

19 See L. Collins (ed.), *Dicey and Morris on the conflict of laws* (13th ed. Sweet & Maxwell: London, 2000), 1288-1289.

20 M. Giuliano & P. Lagarde, 'Report on the Convention on the Law Applicable to Contractual Obligations', [1980] OJ C282/1.

21 Directive 97/7/EC of the European Parliament and of the Council of 20 May 1997 on the protection of consumers in respect of distance contracts [1997] OJ L144/19.

3 CONCLUSION

The Directive on Electronic Commerce[22] makes no provision in relation to jurisdiction or applicable law.[23] Are specific private international law rules required for electronic commerce? In most cases the internet does not raise issues which require different treatment from other contexts. In some cases the law obviously needs to be clarified but litigation may provide satisfactory answers without further reform.

It may be argued that the protection afforded to consumers deters e-commerce. That a small business may be subject to litigation in unpredictable courts subject to consumer protection rules that it is in no position to discover clearly deters business. European Community rules tend to provide a minimum standard for the protection of consumers and a business may still be caught out by rules which go further. English legislation, for example, almost certainly goes further in some respects than is required by the various directives on consumer protection. At a European level, further harmonisation of substantive laws on consumer protection would aid predictability and encourage business. However, the harmonisation of substantive European law is of little assistance if the consumer is situated in, say, Minnesota.

Private international law rules cannot alone provide a perfect solution for both consumers and businesses. A choice needs to be made between protecting the consumer and facilitating business. It is not obvious why this choice should differ according to whether the business is conducted over the internet or by more traditional methods. E-commerce specific rules would lead to inconsistency of treatment and difficult questions of definition (e.g. what is e-commerce?) which would be nearly incapable of being answered without an underlying rationale as to why separate rules were needed.

---

22 Directive 2000/31/EC of the European Parliament and of the Council of 8 June 2000 on certain legal aspects of information society services, in particular electronic commerce, in the Internal Market ('Directive on electronic commerce') [2000] OJ L178/1.

23 Article 1.4.

Law as code, code as law – general remarks on legal requirements engineering*

Aernout Schmidt and Hans Franken

1 Commerce and law in the digital era

In the expression 'e-commerce and law', 'e-commerce' refers to practical forms of trade that are mediated by electronic communication (like the Internet), by electronic processing (like authenticating a message) and by electronic processes (like software agents that are sometimes referred to as intelligent); 'law' refers to the legal aspects involved, not merely contract and commercial law.[1] Although practices of e-commerce stem from the seventies of the last century, the global emergence of Internet in the nineties has nurtured the general feeling of a communication revolution taking place. The Internet revolution brings us into a digital era and poses challenges to the paradigms of law and commerce alike, leaving considerable turbulence in the information industry and considerable room for legal research. The challenges will have to be faced by many, also by legal professionals. Traditional academic legal education may have to adapt itself accordingly. We wonder whether new areas of knowledge should be made available to law students who nourish the ambition to contribute to ordered commerce in the digital era. True to academic tradition, our argumentation starts where legal research fails us.

How to approach the research domain of e-commerce and law is open to discussion. Looking at IT and law in general, we distinguish three problem fields: open texture (i.e. judge-made law by interpretation), legal engineering (the adaptation of IT practices in the law office, for instance) and inherent ambiguity (issued by the difference between the physical world and cyberspace). In 1997, the Dutch government published its leading principle[2] and proposed that what counts as[3] law off line, should count as law on line. This perspective promotes the further interpretative exploitation of open texture[4] in law and seems appropriate when the new behaviour fits into current legal understanding and can be accommodated by case law in the civil-law tradition, like e-mail may fit into regular mail regulation. In 1996/1998, looking at the IT threats and opportunities for the legal profession, Richard Susskind

* Adaptation of the paper presented by Aernout Schmidt at the Leiden-Oxford staff exchange on e-commerce on May 16 and 17, 2001.

1 See for instance the EU Directive 2000/31 EG (8-6-200) on Electronic Commerce (e.g., consideration 40 and articles 12-14).

2 Kabinetsnota *Wetgeving voor de elektronische snelweg* (Communication of the government on legislation for the electronic highway) 1997. This publication has been prepared mainly by legal academics.

3 Meant in the sense of John R. Searle, *The Construction of Social Reality* (Penguin Books, 1995), p. 43.

4 As introduced by F. Waisman (*Verifiability*) in: A. Flew (ed.), *Essays on logic and language*, first series (Oxford, 1951).

H. Snijders, S. Weatherill (eds.), *E-commerce Law*, 117-138

adopted an essentially engineering perspective.[5] This perspective (we baptize it the legal requirements engineering perspective) prompts legal research towards re-engineering legal services and processes. It may be directed to the electronic commerce and law domain, when new services and processes in electronic commerce are developed and deployed under the requirement of legal compliance (like the filter in the Napster case). In 1999, working from a constitutional-review perspective alien to the Dutch legal system, Lawrence Lessig coined the problem of inherent ambiguity, identifying the semantic void sometimes preventing the direct conversion of pre-Internet law into cyberspace regulation.[6] This perspective opens research up towards rethinking the law, specifically for cyberspace, if the old law remains silent to the new behaviour (like during the period of time it has been silent towards digital documents and signatures). In civil-law tradition, inherent ambiguity is accommodated by some attempts to legislation in general and by litigation in individual cases.

The three perspectives represent different positions in the legal system, relevant to electronic commerce. The open-texture perspective often coincides with post hoc legal assessment, as professed by courts, magistrates, solicitors and barristers in litigation. The engineering perspective is appropriate in commerce itself, notably when an e-commerce service is being designed and deployed. The service itself may change the business.7 The relevant legal research in e-commerce is business-oriented and ex ante concerned with modelling the service into an architecture that supports legitimate use. The responsibility risks rest prima facie on the (legal) persons designing and deploying the service, often relying upon legal advice. The latent-ambiguity perspective links tradition with times to come and belongs to litigation in some individual cases but mainly to the legislator – providing enacted rules, addressing areas that may be considered legally void.[8]

By definition, compliance with the law in electronic commerce presupposes applicable law that can be known. New questions of law arise, however, precisely because the IT revolution sustains new forms of civil behaviour unknown to, and not directly fitting in the current legal system. The tempo and the scale of emerging new behaviour in electronic commerce do not only challenge our understanding of their

---

5 Richard Susskind, *The Future of Law: Facing the Challenges of Information Technology* (paperback edition, Oxford University Press, 1998).

6 Lawrence Lessig, *Code and other laws of cyberspace* (Basic Books, New York, 1999); The Lycos Tech glossary (see: <www.webopedia.lycos.com/TERM/c/cyberspace.html>) gives the following definition of cyberspace: 'A metaphor for describing the non-physical terrain created by computer systems. Online systems, for example, create a cyberspace within which people can communicate with one another (via e-mail), do research, or simply window shop. Like physical space, cyberspace contains objects (files, mail messages, graphics, etc.) and different modes of transportation and delivery. Unlike real space, though, exploring cyberspace does not require any physical movement other than pressing keys on a keyboard or moving a mouse. Some programs, particularly computer games, are designed to create a special cyberspace, one that resembles physical reality in some ways but defies it in others. In its extreme form, called virtual reality, users are presented with visual, auditory, and even tactile feedback that makes cyberspace feel real. The term was coined by author William Gibson in his sci-fi novel *Neuromancer* (1984).'

7 Like legal IT-services may change the legal business, as predicted by Susskind 1998 (see note 5).

8 Our legal system of reference is the Dutch system, where the meaning of court decisions is limited to the case at hand and more general legal rules must be legitimated by Parliament.

economics, they also challenge our legal understanding of them and of our ability to adapt the law in time and in a principled way.[9] In electronic commerce and law these areas of legal ambiguity become visible through new IT services. The companies launching them are not just facing economic risks, they may be facing a legal void as well. In these instances legal requirements engineering and inherent ambiguity of the law go hand in hand. There are three predicaments here. One during litigation, interpreting a new world with old law. One for the e-commerce companies, designing services while in the dark about legal constraints (when they are not yet there). The third for the legislator, designing sustainable rules for an area of civil behaviour while in the dark about its shape next year. In litigation, legal professionals must (a) be able to distinguish between open texture and inherent ambiguity; in e-commerce, the company lawyer must (b) know what line separates safe from dangerous IT models when confronted with an area of legal ambiguity; in legislation, the legal professional must (c) know how the development and shape of future e-commercial services will go and will be influenced by the rules being designed. Using recent Dutch case rulings, we will analyse relevance and content of these three areas of knowledge for law students.

Recent Dutch case rulings on e-commerce do not come out of the blue. E-commerce is in many respects the equivalent for electronic data interchange (EDI), the analogous concept in pre-Internet times. Starting from the seventies of the last century, their characteristics can be read from the architectures[10] of computer resources, of the communication infrastructure and of the application design. The architecture of computer resources has moved from mainframes to workstations and personal computers; the architecture of the communication infrastructure has moved from leased lines to Internetworking; the architecture of application design has remained client/server based but is being complemented by peer-to-peer.[11] The architectural evolution of commercial computer messages has been of tremendous importance to the development of EDI and e-commerce – starting with the UN/Edifact[12] initiative and unfolding through SGML, HTML and XML. These linguistic frameworks have supported the development of the artificial languages and dialects that help computers to communicate, negotiate and act independently of direct human intervention, thus moving much of EDI and e-commerce into cyberspace.

Functionally, EDI and e-commerce have developed through emulating existing off-line business practices (business-to-business or B2B) and through emulating mail-ordering services (business-to-consumer or B2C) towards emulating community co-

---

9 *RIAA* v. *Napster* (http://www.riaa.com/pdf/napsterdecision.pdf>) and *United States* v. *Microsoft* (<www.usdoj.gov/atr/cases/ms_index.htm>) are cases in point. See the tremendous amount of, often contradictory, legal opinions on these cases.

10 Architecture plays an important role in Lessig's concept of regulation , Lessig 1999 (see note 6).

11 Mainframes, workstations, leased lines, internetworking, client/server and peer-to-peer are technical concepts lifted from the computer-science domain. Understanding them is necessary to all who want to understand what is going on in cyberspace. Since we expect a large part of e-commerce to realise itself in cyberspace, and our aim is to investigate how much of it should be common ground to legal professionals, we refrain form explaining the 'technical' concepts during our argumentation. For reference, if necessary at all, we will use the exact formulation of the Lycos Tech Glossary (see: <www.webopedia.lycos.com>).

12 See for instance: <www.edicity.com/Resources/EDIFACT.htm>.

operation. Virtual community co-operation uses team groupware to create and maintain services, often on a quid pro quo basis. The Internet has revitalised these ancient business scenarios, as may be found in the open-source movement that has proven to be competitive with Microsoft as well as in the MP3 sharing communities (Napster, Kazaa, MusicCity, etc.) that currently challenge the off-line music industry. Perhaps virtual community co-operation will bring e-commerce to the consumer-to-consumer (C2C) level. It certainly belongs to the domain of e-commerce, since it generates and distributes economic value. It is so new, however, that its economics are not yet understood very well, and legally compliant business models are not yet stable.

EDI and e-commerce have generated many legal activities over time.[13] They include efforts to understand the traditional concepts of agreement and contract formation (between IT-systems), archiving and deeds (paperless), general conditions (handing over), signatures (digital), competition (and closed B2B communities), data protection and crime (in cyberspace), intellectual property (copying, distribution, on computer programs, databases and web methods), freedom of information (web advertising), etc., etc. The methods used range from interpretation (open texture: e.g.digital copying in intellectual property), through functional interpretation (legal requirements engineering: e.g., digital signatures) towards rule construction (legislation: e.g. data protection, intellectual property, cybercrime, telecommunications and e-commerce itself). Apparently, the principle of the Dutch Government, i.e., that what counts as law off line should count as law on line cannot be upheld over time: often, the creativity that is part of the open-texture and engineering solutions to e-commerce related legal questions are followed by the construction of specific cyberspace regulations. And almost as frequently, the resulting laws are out of date even before they have been ratified.

2 OPEN TEXTURE *V* INHERENT AMBIGUITY

RIAA v. *Napster*[14] promises to be a seminal case on virtual community systems in e-commerce. Napster is an information service allowing Internet users to become members of a 'community', sharing music files in MP3 format. The files are exchanged directly between members' computers. An index, or catalogue, is maintained centrally on a server and it is used by members to find out which user has which track of music on offer for downloading for free. The service was created during the first six months of 1999 by a student, Shawn Fanning. On 1 June he launched the beta test version, making it available to 30 friends and acquaintances. A short time later, millions of music tracks were shared by millions of users all over the world and the American music industry became uncomfortable, so much, that the RIAA and others started a lawsuit on contributory copyright infringement. The judge ordered Napster Inc. to create a filter, preventing the sharing of copyrighted music

13 As for instance described by R.E. van Esch, *Electronic Data Interchange en het vermogensrecht* (EDI and property law) (Deventer, W.E.J. Tjeenk Willink, 1999) and by Michael Chissick and Alistair Kelman, *Electronic Commerce: law and practice* (London, Sweet & Maxwell, 2000).

14 See <www.napster.com/pressroom/legal.html>.

tracks in the community, by checking them against a list provided by the RIAA. The filter was built, did not function faultlessly and by August 2001 the Napster community was virtually dead.

Kazaa is a service, functionally superior to the Napster service. It not only supports audio-file sharing, but also document-, video- and program file sharing. Its architecture is also slightly different: there is no central server with a catalogue. The Kazaa catalogue is constructed dynamically on member computers from the information supplied by members. The Kazaa service is freely made available by Kazaa BV as a program file. On 30 December 2001 there were '558250 users on line, sharing 80660K files (444720.0 GB).' Compared with the blooming period of Napster, much seems to have remained the same. Most members of the Napster community have moved on to Kazaa or a similar service and the RIAA has initiated a lawsuit against Kazaa in the USA. In the Netherlands, the District Court of Amsterdam issued a summary judgment on 28 November 2001.[15] Litigants were Kazaa BV, providing a proper peer-to-peer service for file sharing, and Buma/Stemra, defending the Dutch music industry. The initiative in the case was Kazaa's; its aim was to force Buma/Stemra into an agreement on copyright compensation. Buma/Stemra claimed in reverse that Kazaa should stop copyright infringement through the use of its service forthright. In the judgment, judge Orobio de Castro, ordered, amongst other things, as follows:

> ... orders Kazaa, within 14 days after ratification of this judgment, to take such measures that copyright infringement, distributing and copying music works that belong to the Buma/Stemra repertoire, using computer programs made available by Kazaa, is no longer possible, under forfeit of NLG 100,000.- per day with a maximum of NLG 2,000,000.-...

On January 31, 2002, the notice was long overdue. Kazaa had filed the appeal case and was told in an intermediary summary judgment that the forfeit would not be postponed.[16] The Kazaa business was sold to an Australian company.

In our opinion the first-instance Kazaa judgment is ruled from an inherent-ambiguity position, and not argued very well at that. We give the arguments exchanged. Buma/Stemra stated:

> Buma/Stemra claims that Kazaa, by means of its computer program, infringes copyrights. The making available of music files by users to all other users constitutes making them available to the public in the sense of the Dutch Copyright Act. Downloading these music files, made accessible to other users by Kazaa, constitutes infringing multiplication, not excluded in article 16b of the Dutch Copyright Act.

Kazaa defended itself by arguing:

> Kazaa challenges Buma/Stemra's claim that it infringes copyrights by making its computer program available to the public. As an intermediary party, Kazaa does not copy or distribute music files. Neither is there complicity or liability, because Kazaa acts as a producer of the computer program proper, and cannot be held responsible for the behaviour of its users.

15 See http: <www.rechtspraak.nl >LJN-nummer: AD6395 Zaaknr: KG 01/2264 OdC (in Dutch).

16 See http: <www.rechtspraak.nl> LJN-nummer: AD8749 Zaaknr: KG 02/0105 OdC (in Dutch).

Judge Orobio de Castro straightforwardly decided as follows:

> First it must be put that Kazaa infringes copyright, by giving its users the means, through its program, to download music files without licence.

That was it, no further arguments were provided. However, several observations have to be made. The Dutch Copyright Act does not accommodate contributory infringement (as is the case in the USA). Consequently, the judge has interpreted Kazaa's behaviour as direct copyright infringement. The provision of an instrument (a computer program) by the producer and distributor of that instrument, which may be used by the recipient to infringe, is seen as infringement proper. We do not think that reading the facts in this way can be classified as making use of open texture validly. Too many instances of the provision of instruments that may be used for good as well as for bad are kept outside the responsibility of the provider in the Dutch legal system. Hammers (murder) and copiers (copyright infringement), radio transmitters (copyright infringement) and nursery lights (weed) can be produced and distributed without the distributor becoming responsible for the use they are put to. Even fire arms are in this category, although there is a law prohibiting their free production and distribution. Making the maker of an instrument responsible for its use simply does not fit into the Dutch legal system very well. Apparently judge Orobio de Castro has chosen an inherent-ambiguity position, perceiving an 'empty space' in the law, abused by Kazaa. Unfortunately, he considered his opinion self-evident and left us in the dark about his reasoning. Perhaps even more unfortunate, his judgment may affect legal security in the software industry: it warns that possible abuse should be an important issue during design, implementation and deployment of computer programs in general, including e-commerce services. Consequently, it may be felt in the industry that possible abuse must be foreseen, and, if so, the development of tools otherwise considered beneficiary must be prevented. Imagine the development of e-mail services aborted for fear of their possible abuse.

On March 28, 2002, the Amsterdam Court of Appeal in the Kazaa-case ruled as follows:[17]

> ... Furthermore, the Court of Appeal mentions that Kazaa rightly opposes the first-instance ruling that first it must be put that Kazaa infringes copyright by giving its users the means, through its program, to download music files without licence. As far as copyright-infringing behaviour is at stake at all, the behaviour is performed by the users of the computer program and not by Kazaa. Making available the means to distribute or copy copyrighted works does not in itself constitute distribution or multiplication of those works. Neither is it the case, at least it cannot be assumed for the present, that Kazaa's computer program is exclusively used for downloading copyright-protected works. Kazaa has shown on appeal a large number of examples of works that have permission of the author, have fallen in the public domain, do not enjoy copyright protection at all or are legally excepted from copyright protection. Moreover, Huizer in his 'expert opinion' does provide examples of other uses. Buma/Stemra may state that the only, at least only essential, function of Kazaa's computer program is to provide users with the means to exchange copyright-protected works, but this claim is contradicted by Kazaa with force of arguments and is not elucidated further by Buma/Stemra at all. That the other use is meaningless counts doubtlessly for Buma/Stemra, but that does not imply its irrelevance to those other users. ...

17 See <www.rechtspraak.nl> LJN-nummer: AE0805 Zaaknr: 1370/01SKG (in Dutch).

Clearly, the Court of Appeal takes the open-texture approach and is brought to a reverse decision. Where is the line between inherent-ambiguity reasoning as used in the first instance and open-texture reasoning as used on appeal?

Prima facie, questions about the line between open texture and inherent ambiguity in e-commerce are no different from questions about that division in any other area. Presumably, its location is affected by the role and position of court judgments in the legal system under investigation. In the Netherlands, the role and position of courts forbid them to judge the legitimacy of enacted rules, prevent them from judging contra legem in individual cases, order them to give judgment in individual cases even if relevant enacted rules are nonexistent and deny them the right to formulate general rules. As a corollary, Dutch jurisprudence expects an open-texture line of reasoning, if valid, to take priority over inherent-ambiguity argumentation: the judge may not assume the role of the legislator. The importance of the distinction between open texture and inherent ambiguity lies in the necessity in the last case to employ non-legal argumentation to solve legal disputes. Naturally, the issue is not reserved for Dutch law and Dutch courts. It boils down to three daunting questions: what counts as valid legal reasoning in an open-texture context, what counts as valid legal reasoning in an inherent-ambiguity context and what separates the open-texture context from the inherent-ambiguity context.

What lines of legal reasoning are valid has been researched and commented upon extensively. It is not our aim to enter into the swamp of academic dispute in this area of jurisprudence. For making our point here we need some practical characteristics to break down the field heuristically, so we can go on with the main argument as soon as possible. We have chosen to use two dimensions for this, irreverently and mercilessly[18] borrowed from the work of the constitutional law scholar Bobbitt[19] and the psychologist Fodor[20] respectively. Bobbitt analysed the types of arguments used during the history of constitutional review in the USA and comes up with a limitative[21] list: historical (addressing the intentions of the rule makers), textual (addressing the present sense of the rule wording), doctrinal (addressing the principles and relations derived from precedent), prudential (self-consciously addressing role and position of the party or institution that is reasoning), structural (addressing implicit meaning from the existence and role of legal institutions) and ethical (arguments addressing the ethos of a22 jurisdiction or politeia). Fodor is interested in natural and in artificial intelligence and in how human knowledge representation relates to knowledge representation in IT. He finds the distinctions of abstraction layers as a basic similarity and considers the positioning of abstraction layers relative to reasoning of fundamental importance. Imposing Fodor's abstraction layers upon legal argument we distinguish six layers: beliefs (like in a free market, the ten commandments), prin-

18 Irreverently, because put to use in a very blunt, practical and generalizing way that does not and cannot respect the finesses of their fine work.

19 Philip Bobbitt, *Constitutional Fate – theory of the constitution* (Oxford University Press, 1982).

20 J.A. Fodor, *Psychosemantics* (MIT press, 1987).

21 Despite his claim not to be exhaustive on p. 8, the exercise proposed on p. 94 and 95 suggests the opposite (Bobbitt 1982, see note 19).

22 Here we generalize over Bobbitt's typification – he mentions the ethos of *American* polity.

ciples (like in human rights, in the constitution), rules (like in acts, for instance, democratically formulating exceptions to human rights), policies (like in administrative plans, interchange agreements and common-law precedent), individual judgments (like in civil-law precedent, in transactions) and facts (making up the facts of a case). Types of argument content can be related to levels of abstraction in the following framework:

History	Text	Doctrine	Prudence	Structure	Ethics
Beliefs					
Principles					
Rules					
Policies					
Judgments					
Facts					

Table 1: Abstraction levels and argument types

The framework helps to present our heuristic distinction of valid from invalid legal reasoning in the different contexts. First of all, the different levels of abstraction represent different sources for legal arguments. In an open-texture context, only facts, judgments, policies, rules and principles are valid sources for argument, and only the reasoning is valid, which brings facts within the constraints of valid judgments, that are within the constraints of valid policies, that are within the constraints of valid rules, that are within the constraints of valid principles. In normal circumstances, beliefs do not provide valid sources for legal arguments in an open-texture context and neither are ethical arguments admissible – anyway, in a stable politeia, arguments at the belief level and arguments of the ethical type are most often coherent with valid legal reasoning.

If not – when an open-texture judgment is incoherent with beliefs and ethics, when valid open-texture reasoning is not possible at all – then there is a case to be made for a shift in perspectives and try inherent-ambiguity reasoning. Valid inherent-ambiguity reasoning allows, if necessary, ethical arguments at all levels and allows, if necessary, common beliefs to provide a closure for reasoning.

Inherent ambiguity presents itself when there is a dispute that cannot be solved using valid open-texture legal reasoning. This often happens when IT-solutions are outside reasonable interpretation of the facts in traditional law, but somehow need to be dragged into the legal system. Lessig shows some wonderful examples in American constitutional law and we will encounter an example in Dutch law presently. Our (heuristic) claim is that legal reasoning in an inherent-ambiguity context may validly use ethical arguments and common beliefs. In Dutch jurisprudence,

Administration	Accommodation
Accessibility	Transparency
Confidentiality	Flexibility
Reliability[23]	
Authenticity	

Table 2: Franken's principles

Franken[24] has proposed six ethical principles to guide reasoning about the use of IT in cases of legal ambiguity. In e-commerce cases, they rest upon two beliefs: (1) that a business must at all times keep a valid administration and (2) that legal rules, if generated by future law, must be accommodated in future business procedure. We mention these principles in Table 2. They were introduced in 1993 and have in the meantime become more or less self-evident. These principles can be seen as a specification of the general principles of law which are applied in every off-line law practice. In the 'real' world we live with principles of tort law, principles of contract law, principles of reasonable government decision-making etc. We can point at legal notions as the fair play principle and audite et alterem partem in procedural law, ne bis in idem in criminal law, carefulness in operations and the nemo auditur rule in civil law, the prohibition of détournement de pouvoir in administrative law etc. These principles can be specified and applied to the technical and the societal demands of IT relations and will give the practitioner, the judge and the legislator the possibility to express a rational consideration of interests and recognition of values.

We look back at the three cases summarily presented above for illustration. In the Napster case, in the USA, contributory copyright infringement could be validly argued with open-texture reasoning, because it is a legal concept in the USA at the rule level and the facts fit the rules. The Napster software was made with the intention to use it for sharing music files, also, and mostly, copyrighted music files. The architecture of the service allowed Napster Inc. to make an end to naïve, abusive music sharing by implementing a filter in the server software. The remedies ordered by the judge, making the music industry provide a list with copyrighted works and making Napster Inc. implement a filter, preventing the sharing of listed music files, are generally considered within the limits of valid legal ruling in the USA.

Had the Napster case been filed in the Netherlands, its result could have been different. The concept of contributory copyright infringement does not exist in Dutch copyright law and the available legal notions of tort and criminal complicity would have been very difficult to prove and use successfully. It seems reasonable that an open-texture result would have been considered contradictory to common beliefs and commercial ethics by many. In Dutch polity, the principled way to handle the

23 This principle is often referred to as 'integrity.' Reliability (claiming a computer service to behave in accordance with its specifications) implies integrity, which often has the restricted connotation of messages not being corrupted during communication.

24 H. Franken, 'Juridisch Theoretische achtergronden' (Jurisprudential background) in: H. Franken, H.W.K. Kaspersen & A.H. de Wild (eds.), *Recht en computer* (Law and Computer) (4th edition, Kluwer, 2001, p. 33-74.

case would have been to judge in accordance with existing law, generating sufficient public indignation to prompt new legislature. However, our current preference for what has become known as our *poldermodel* (i.e. consensus model), resulting in many deviations from principled methods, might have induced the court to settle things directly via precedent, venturing to express a new policy.[25] It seems to us that judge Orobio de Castro has tried to do just that in the Kazaa case in the first instance. An ethical principle that may have been behind his judgment could be the lack of flexibility of the Kazaa program. Once made available to the public, it drifted outside the influence of the distributor, can still be distributed freely by others and cannot directly[26] be adapted by the Kazaa company for future use, if future law would require it. This issue is of great importance: Lessig's digital commons, including the open-source movements, do depend on architectures that prevent influence by the distributor. In the Kazaa appeal, a more principled approach has been applied.

We wonder what the American legal system will in its turn make of the Kazaa case; due to its multifunctionality and its true peer-to-peer architecture, it may be much more difficult than in the Napster case to construe contributory infringement from an open-texture position in a valid way.

Legal professionals handling e-commerce using open-texture reasoning need to be able to decide on the legal meaning of legal concepts in trade law, for business situations, which are realized with a significant support of IT processes. From a trade-law perspective, we summarised these concepts by mentioning legal areas of interest: the traditional concepts of agreement and contract formation (between IT-systems), archiving and deeds (paperless), general conditions (handing over), signatures (digital), competition (and closed B2B communities), data protection and crime (in cyberspace), intellectual property (copying, distribution, on computer programs, databases and web methods), freedom of information (web advertising). Legal professionals that address e-commerce issues need to know what tools and models are available in a standard way and what their functions are in these legal areas, of interest to the e-commerce and law community. A random selection of items they need to know about is: virus scanners and firewalls, about web-browsers, search engines and web servers, about databases, about encryption, security, intranets and virtual private networks, about chat functions and groupware, about mail functions and pay functions, about logging and testing, about content/workflow management functions, about content communication standards and transport communication standards, about communication scenarios, about TCP/IP and ports, about agents and worms and sniffers, about media players and operating systems, about client-server and peer-to-peer architectures, about objects, messages and methods. Not at the level of IT professionals, but at the level of sufficiently understanding them functionally,[27]

25 In this, it seems that the principled divide between common-law and civil-law systems is reduced, as widely defended in the literature.

26 This seems more of a theoretical than of a practical problem: IT services are constantly adapted and *versioning* of services is general practice. Indirectly, flexibility could be implemented through adaptations in later versions of the program.

27 Many of these have been treated that way in A.H.J. Schmidt and L. Mommers, 'Informatie en communicatie' (Information and Communication) in: H. Franken, H.W.K. Kaspersen & A.H. de Wild (eds.), *Recht en computer* (Law and Computer) (4th edition, Kluwer 2001), p. 1-31.

sufficiently to be able to identify their relevance and position (as in Table 1) in open-texture and inherent-ambiguity legal reasoning. We cannot yet relate these IT-functions with the legal areas of interest mentioned in an orderly manner. First we will have to break down the engineering approach in a similar manner as we have been doing with the open-texture approach in the current chapter.

3 SAFE *V* DANGEROUS BUSINESS MODELS: COMPLIANCE ENGINEERING

The Netherlands Association of Real Estate Brokers (NVM) has a web service that lets house hunters specify their requirements and subsequently provides a complying list of real-estate objects for sale. In the back-end of the service operates a database that is maintained by the NVM members collectively. The service is open to all and free of charge. The Dutch newspaper De Telegraaf has subsequently designed, implemented and deployed a web service named El Cheapo. One of the functions of El Cheapo is similar to the NVM service. Moreover, El Cheapo employs an intermediary software agent that automatically communicates with the NVM service and presents the NVM results as part of its reply to the user's request. Although the presentation of the results does specify its sources, and although further inquiries about specific real-estate objects are handled through direct linking to the NVM data repository, the NVM organisation was not amused by El Cheapo and filed suit. The resulting litigation between NVM and De Telegraaf (we later refer to it as the El Cheapo case) has thus far been through three stages. A first-instance summary judgment by the The Hague court awarded the NVM claim of database right infringement, the appeal summary judgment by the The Hague Court of Appeal awarded the De Telegraaf claim and the cassation judgment by the Supreme Court of the Netherlands redirected the case back to the appeal-court level with instructions that seem to be in favour of the NVM. The El Cheapo case is still work in progress, it seems, and in an area of legal insecurity. In this chapter we adopt the legal requirements engineering perspective in order to examine the knowledge needed by the legal professional that has the task to advise De Telegraaf during design, implementation and deployment of the El Cheapo service. The task implies *ex ante* knowledge of the legal risks involved and it implies careful tracking of the (al)location of responsibilities and liabilities during design, implementation and deployment of the service as well.

Imagine being employed by De Telegraaf in an early stage of the El Cheapo project – even before a functional design of the service has been made. Imagine that the chief executive officer of De Telegraaf has, for some time now, been pregnant with an idea that will bind a considerable amount of readers: an Internet service with houses for sale, where consumers can specify wishes, and where the service in reply will provide information on the available houses for sale. As a major countrywide daily newspaper, De Telegraaf has a famous weekly special with advertisements of real estate for sale, it could become the backbone source of information for the service. Additional information can be found on the Internet, where several sources on real estate for sale are in the offering for free. The CEO makes a sketch of a business plan and decides that the service is economically feasible. He attracts an IT business as contractor and concurrently appoints you to provide legal advice throughout the project, to be presented as a part of the milestone reports he is to receive. To prepare your work plans, indeed, in order to do your work professionally, you will have to know what the milestones are, what issues your reports are to address and in what context they will be presented.

IT projects have in the past often proven difficult to manage. During the sixties and seventies of the previous century, millions and millions of any currency have been lost in failed IT projects and a considerable effort has been made in computer science to construct effective knowledge about methods that reduce the risks in IT development projects. The work has converged in 'unified' heuristics for the planning and realisation of computer services. A huge heap of learned writing has emerged in this area, ranging from addressing the formal (e.g., Codd's[28] famous *relational data model* and Dijkstra's[29] almost equally famous *structured programming*) via method comparison and fusion (e.g., Wieringa's *requirements engineering*)[30] and object orientation (e.g. Jacobson, Booch and Rumbaugh's[31] trilogy) to finally including the psychological and organisational (e.g. Schreiber et. al.'s[32] *knowledge engineering*). The tremendous amount of work in this area has resulted in much better manageable development projects, resting on a stable paradigm – so much so, that in the IT world specialization has resulted. It makes good sense to be knowledgeable about the paradigm as well as about the specialists if you want your advice to make any impact (or even sense) in the non-legal culture where the decisions are, and have to be, made.

The paradigm is treacherously simple: if you want to develop a computer service, you take the idea, make a model of it in natural language and translate that to more formal models until it is a working computer program. Unlike developing a subway system, where the idea will also be modelled into formalities, it does not need to be realised in tunnels and steel. The seductive and wonderful thing about the most formal model in the IT development process is that it can be fed into a simple, generic machine and will spring into life forthright – operating. Then and there, the model is its own object, so to speak. In this line of reasoning, the meaning of a compiled computer program is purely referential to its own behaviour. No wonder that computer scientists tend to be reluctant towards anti-realist philosophy entering their discipline: if the computer does not behave in accordance with its program, it assumes a contextual meaning (e.g., computer behaviour when the power supply gets out of order) that is simply wrong – the program does not show its *true* behaviour. This attitude is firmly rooted in the IT discipline, and rightly so – be it not without its drawbacks. Rightly so, because in the IT business much depends on trust in proven products, and ceteris paribus, software products can be proven in a formal way. Dangerously so, because ceteris tend not to remain paribus, and because the meaning of a computer program in a social world is rather its behaviour and use

28 E. F. Codd, 'A Relational Model of Data for Large Shared Data Banks', *Communications of the ACM* 13 /6 (1970), p. 377-387.

29 O,-J. Dahl, E.W. Dijkstra & C.A.R. Hoare, Structured programming (Academic press, 1972).

30 R.J. Wieringa, *Requirements Engineering: Frameworks for Understanding* (Wiley, 1996).

31 The most relevant of these is: I. Jacobson, G. Booch & J. Rumbaugh, *The Unified Software Development Process* (Addison-Wesley, 1999).

32 G. Schreiber, H. Akkermans & O. Anjewierden, *Knowledge Engineering and Management* (MIT Press, 2001).

related to the original idea in an organisational context, than to the most formal model in the context of an operating computer. The history of IT development methods has, without forgetting about the formal meaning, gradually shown additional attention to the organisational meaning of the service being developed. The mainstream paradigm of the IT world is now also concerned with the construction of a working model of an idea, as used in an organisation. Herewith it has shed much of its simplicity. The literature mentioned unfolds the modelling process into descriptive and operational themes. Addressing these themes has become good practice in the IT world and may consequently be of importance to the practitioner's advice.

The descriptive themes in IT service development are best understood as chapters[33] in the report, describing the model of the idea under realisation. There are five chapters: on the contextual organisation (e.g. De Telegraaf, Internet, newspaper publics), on processes and tasks performed by the organisation (e.g. publishing news and commentaries, specials, advertisements and information on real estate for sale), on agents that perform these tasks and their qualification as either automated (e.g.web-publishing real estate for sale) or not (e.g. writing commentaries), on the communication between the agents – where communication between automated agents is fully formalised (e.g., between web servers and databases) and the description of mixed communication gives the user interfaces (e.g. between users and web services) and on the knowledge that the different agents need to perform their tasks (e.g. about the information format in other web services to be used automatically). Together, these chapters provide the model of the idea to be realised in its context; we name it the *contextual model.* Where and when the legal paragraphs in the different chapters are due is a question we will have to address later, because we have to sort out some procedural aspects first.

The contextual model of an IT service under development is a moving target. It starts in very general and summary terms as the sketch of a business model. It finishes in extremely formal and specific tones, often incorporating the source code of executable computer programs in its appendices. As the descriptive element of the paradigm, the contextual model will reflect growing stages, closely related to the process of development in a procedural sense.

The first effective procedural view (again developed in the seventies of the previous century) of the generalised IT development process was represented by the waterfall metaphor, breaking down the work in an almost self-evident sequential chain of IT sub-projects – the general idea being that an information analysis must be available in order to make a functional model, that implementation should not start before the functional model had been completed, that testing could not take place before implementation, that the service should not be deployed before it had been

33 These chapters have been analyzed and described very well by Schreiber 2001 (see note 32) for academic education. They need 439 pages. Within the constraints of this contribution, we treat them like we treated Bobbitt and Fodor: irreverently, because put to use in a very blunt, practical and generalizing way that does not and cannot respect the finesses of their fine work, which is the result of a continuous research line started in 1982 by Wielinga and Breuker at the research group on artificial intelligence of Amsterdam University.

tested and that maintenance of the service should be considered only after substantial experience of use had been gained. Again, the waterfall metaphor is of a treacherously simple nature. It has proven to be of great value, but has in the meantime proven to be almost impossible to uphold in real-world situations. Consequently, the procedural development paradigm has unfolded into themes rather than sequential subprojects. As we see it, six of them have settled in the nucleus of unified methods: requirements analysis, functional design, implementation and graphical design, testing, deployment and maintenance.

Requirements analysis addresses the specification of the initial idea in a manner supporting contract formation between the initiating company and the contractor of the IT development project. From a legal orientation, several kaleidoscopically scattered aspects require attention. First, the context for agreement formation should be valid – implying clearly defined responsibilities and sufficient available information to support valid agreement. The initial contextual model is performative here. Requirements analysis thus unfolds the initial idea in context, addressing all chapters in terms of the functional requirements that the initiating company wishes for and the contractor promises to meet and deliver. Naturally, one would insist on a clear wording of the promises made, since the contracting parties will almost always show considerable asymmetries in their knowledge – the company CEO seldom being a computer scientist and the contractor seldom being *au courant* with the intricacies of the business it will make the service for. The requirements analysis theme thus aims first of all at elevating their understanding to make true agreement possible. Second, as legal advisor of the initiating company you would consider the risks involved and the relevance of legal solutions to possible problems. As a legal advisor you, too, will have to understand what is going on here. For instance, the functional use of publicly available and free Internet services provided by others like the NVM will have become visible at this stage and it is your task to push the breaks and explain the legal risks involved. It may well be that De Telegraaf will discontinue the project if it considers these risks unacceptable. Third, you should prevent falling in the natural trap of assuming that the requirements analysis theme, including contract formation, is definitive before further steps are taken. Very often, almost every time, the development process itself propels parties' understanding into progression and will unveil the need for contract adaptation. Moreover, the IT world around has not frozen into immobility during the development process and it is highly probable that new and better tools become available during the ride. As a legal advisor you should anticipate and choose contract wording accordingly. Fourth, you should be aware that the contractor will almost always need subcontractors. Information asymmetries will be incumbent there also.

The IT world has developed several specialisms that are suitable for the themes under investigation. The requirements analysis theme is often addressed by a mixture of information- and organisation-analyst expertise; the functional design theme is often looked after by systems-analyst expertise; implementation and graphical design by programming and human-machine interface expertise respectively; testing has to be approached from the formal angle by application programmers, and from the organisational angle by a mixed team of expected users and representatives of

Information analyst
Application programmer
Systems analyst
Systems programmer

Table 3: IT specialisms

the initiating company and the contractor; deployment is a completely different cup of tea, handled by network and system programming specialists; activating the maintenance theme either means breaking open the initial contracts during the ride, or implies starting a new development process altogether. Breaking down the IT development process into themes naturally leads to the appointment of different specialists responsible for different themes. Because addressing the themes cannot be usefully organised sequentially, it should be organised in parallel project groups, with clear conditions and concurrency points (milestones) for inter-theme communication. Your advice to incorporate these conditions and milestones into the relevant agreements between contractors and subcontractors makes sense, because the current breakdown is in accordance with what has become good practice in IT and may consequently be used in a normative manner.

The *functional design* theme addresses the functional specification of tasks to be performed by agents that are themselves or communicate with electronic agents in the service under development. In this theme, the focus is on computer applications, the context is reduced to users. As a result, the functional design theme will add agent-related content to the chapters of the contextual model, and in a semi-formal format at that. After all, functional designs tend to be jotted down in the unified modelling language (IT people say UML). You will be inclined to leave the theme to the specialists. Several legal issues may need your attention, however. First, because functional models are more formally expressed than requirements. This simply implies loss of context-oriented semantic wealth and gain of computer-oriented semantic accuracy, and consequently many choices have to be made. This may lead to discrepancies that should be herded outside the danger area wherein the resulting service becomes unacceptable. An agreement on prototyping the design for evaluation might be taken into consideration. Second, because communication amongst electronic agents and communication between users and electronic agents may raise issues of standardisation, privacy, intellectual property and, using ethical arguments, issues of accessibility, confidentiality, reliability and authenticity. Here it is, that you will have to provide important advice (and that you may find a second chance if you missed out on the database protection issue during requirements analysis). Here it is also, that you may provide information that can help the design to result in a legally compliant service. Here it is then, that you start fiddling with the design models and your advice becomes compliance engineering. We will address compliance engineering separately, after completing our current breakdown of the IT development process.

The *implementation and graphical design* theme is concerned with two disciplines. Implementation is a programmer and system engineering activity, extending the contextual model in the areas of the design theme. No single service is developed from scratch, nowadays. Using UML during design shows an object oriented approach, which has been prompted by the urge not to have to redesign functional program objects that have been made available elsewhere. There is a huge reservoir of available objects out there, which is continually being supplemented. Before coding new objects, research is necessary for available resources. Decisions must be made about using them and about acquiring the rights to do so, if necessary. You could recommend reviewing and discussing these decisions in an early stage. The graphical design theme is performed by graphical artists and adds to the contextual model in the area of agent-user communication. Graphical design is extremely important and needs to be approved by the principal contractor separately. Self-evidently, the legal issues of intellectual property must be addressed in your advice.

The *testing* theme is complex and is legally important: acceptance or refusal of the resulting service belongs to it. In the requirements engineering theme the conditions for acceptance and refusal are set, initially, and, if necessary, reset, when the initial agreement is adapted. Pilot testing of the design models may be agreed upon. Agreements about procedures for conflict resolution are necessary.

The *deployment* theme addresses the issue of live hosting and maintaining the service on servers in the network. It adds heavily to the contextual model in the organisational area. The issue is very much technical and systems and network engineers will do the work. The knowledge asymmetries will traditionally be huge. Legally, the use of service level agreements has become standard. They regard many issues pertaining to interchange agreements. The problems of scaling should be addressed also if there is any chance of the service becoming a countrywide or worldwide success. In an internet context, things can get out of control really quickly.

The *maintenance* theme has two sides. One side aims at improving the quality of the service and may be realised through closure of the current development process and restart after relevant experience has been gained during operational use. The other side is concerned with continuity – which may be challenged by changing circumstances in the context (new versions of TCP/IP or HTML become popular, the original contractor is out of business, software objects used in implementation or network and hosting service providers are discontinued). Two issues may be legally addressed here: (1) contractual provisions about making available the source code may be of solace in some of these eventualities and (2) requiring the parties active in the themes to provide adequate documentation, thus contributing to the knowledge chapter of the contextual model and to the ethical principles of flexibility and transparency.

The reader who has persisted thus far may ask himself why there is no theme devoted to the operational use of the service. In our breakdown, this issue is dispersed over several themes and chapters. The deployment theme addresses the service

other. As Lessig pointed out, the way these layers are constricted by intellectual property law may influence the manner in which new services may be developed and deployed. The Kazaa and El Cheapo cases make that clear, too. The other area of legal influence is likely to be competition law, considering the interdependencies. No wonder that competition law is the main issue in telecom regulation.

Another interesting aspect that can be shown through Table 4 concerns the areas of consumer-to-consumer e-commerce. These areas will be populated by peer-to-peer applications. Although in our current legal system we have plenty of attention for consumer protection in the business-to-consumer areas, consumer-to-consumer e-commerce is new. The main legal issues it will generate seem to be: When should consumer-to-consumer e-commerce be treated as business-to-business, when as business-to-consumer and when as a sui generis business relationship? How can business-to-business regulation be upheld under the numerical explosion of 'businesses' in consumer-to-consumer e-commerce? Are the infrastructure services at lower levels to be considered as 'essential facilities'? Again, the Kazaa case gives us an indication how these issues may unfold in the future.

In *Code as Law*, Lessig brings four regulating forces to the fore: legal, social, economic and architectural. He focuses on the architectural regulating powers of code in areas of communication and application. These powers are emerging *per se*, through e-commercial practice: code as law, as it were, closely related to our legal-requirements-engineering position; they are emerging through law as well, leading to new implementations of regulatory architectures in code: law as code, as it were, closely related to the inherent-ambiguity position. His argumentation leads to a reserved approach to legislation for cyberspace, to a warning against naïvely translating traditional intellectual property law for cyberspace and the legal engineering of a 'commons' in cyberspace (where e.g. the open-source movement lives), leaving room for free interaction and cooperation in communities. In *The future of ideas*, Lessig elaborates on the threats of intellectual property rights for cyberspace and argues for 'commons' at the physical level, at both code levels and at the content level, proposing changes in property law on the fly. His view on the future of cyberspace is dim, because of the direction e-commerce is taking under current law.

In our opinion, Lessig is right and wrong. Concerning the 'commons' we fully agree. Concerning the threats by current intellectual property rights for the commons, we heartily disagree: current intellectual property rights shape and protect the commons. To translate the problem to the El Cheapo case level: nobody prevents those that have real estate for sale to start a community web service functionally equivalent to and content-wise better than the NVM service. Very successful services of the type exist – in the Netherlands notably <www.tweakers.net> as a hardware and software marketplace. In our opinion, it is perfectly all right when creator-related additional value is protected, as long as community-related additional value can be published in the commons and can be protected against being usurped by commercial free-riders that bring it outside the commons with no value added.

With these arguments in mind, we return to the future of e-commerce on cyberspace, from the inherent-ambiguity perspective. The central, practical problem in both the Kazaa case and the El Cheapo case are related to the possibility for parties to know whether a file or a record in a database is actively protected by intellectual property law or not. If this information were available for the agents searching the Internet, they could behave compliantly. When the information is not available, using and re-using information that is freely published on the Internet may prove to be infringement. These risks do hamper the evolution of ideas and services alike. It is not the interpretation of 'substantial use' that will solve these problems in general, nor will fiddling with copyright and database right protection periods solve much. Transparency of the protection status of published content will. We need the ©-sign back, in a digital version, and several more signs to label various database protection levels and intellectual property licencing practices.

For the time being, these labels have not been generally accepted in practice. It may be within the power of the legislator to introduce them. Of eminent importance for the future of the Internet will be the choice about the default status of any digitally published unlabelled piece of information. A free default will fit nicely into the traditional ethos of cyberspace. Furthermore, protection by labelling will not be very laborious or difficult in e-commerce. Instead of making further data-protection law, we would advise the legislator to enact a simple cyberspace labelling paragraph in the Copyright and Database acts.

5 Required knowledge

We wondered whether new areas of knowledge should be made available to law students who nourish the ambition to contribute to ordered commerce in the digital era. We distinguished three different perspectives for legal reasoning by legal professionals: the open-texture perspective for litigation, the legal engineering perspective for legal advisors and the inherent-ambiguity perspective for rule making. We provided a unified framework of themes and chapters, providing the contextual model of an IT service and describing the basic architecture of good IT development practice. We sketched the structure of e-commerce on cyberspace, using four service levels and three business types. We finally used the Kazaa case and the El Cheapo case to analyse the knowledge required by the legal professionals involved. For litigation professionals, we found it necessary to be knowledgeable about the legal meaning of existing IT functions. For the advising professional, we found it necessary to be knowledgeable about the legal risks that will be relevant to future IT functions. For the legislator, we found it necessary to be knowledgeable about ethos of and principles for cyberspace. The legal professional, contributing to ordered commerce in the legal era, must know enough of IT to be able to read and understand the analysis and design themes of contextual models and to be able to detect the legal issues involved. He must furthermore understand the ethos of the Internet, and the finesses of the ethical principles involved. We apprehend that an analogous argument can be made for legal professionals that are directing their attention to e-government. We further expect that, ten years from now, commerce will have mainly become *e*-commerce and government will have mainly become *e*-government. We think that academic legal education should accommodate these needs.

List of contributors and editors

- Roderick Bagshaw is fellow of Magdalen College, Oxford University
- Rob van Esch is professor of E-Commerce Law and fellow of the E. M. Meijers Institute, Leiden University, and senior manager of the Legal and tax department of Rabobank Nederland
- Hans Franken is professor of IT Law and fellow of the E.M. Meijers Institute, Leiden University
- Josh Holmes is lecturer in Law at University College London
- Bronwen Morgan is Harold Woods Research Fellow at Wadham College and Centre for Socio-Legal Studies, Oxford University
- Cyril van der Net is former lecturer of IT Law at Leiden University, and legal advisor at the Dutch Ministry of Justice
- Hans Nieuwenhuis is professor of Civil Law and fellow of the E.M. Meijers Institute, Leiden University
- Aernout Schmidt is associate professor of IT Law and fellow of the E.M. Meijers Institute, Leiden University
- Henk Snijders is professor of Civil Law and fellow of the E.M. Meijers Institute, Leiden University
- Robert Stevens is fellow of Lady Margaret Hall, Oxford University, and a barrister
- Dirk Visser is lecturer in intellectual property law and fellow of the E.M. Meijers Institute, Leiden University, and *advocaat* and *procureur* in Amsterdam
- Stephen Weatherill is Jacques Delors Professor of EC Law and fellow of Somerville College, Oxford University

Subject Index